WHAT I LEARNED UNDER THE SUN

What I Learned under the Sun

My Unbelievable True Life

"You have to have faith even against seemingly insurmountable odds."

Kyle L. Coon

Copyright © 2010 by Kyle L. Coon.

Library of Congress Control Number: 2010908128
ISBN: Hardcover 978-1-4535-1501-3
Softcover 978-1-4535-1500-6
Ebook 978-1-4535-1502-0

This book, or parts thereof, may not be reproduced in any form, stored in a retrieval system, or transmitted in any form by any means—electronic, mechanical, photocopy, recording, or otherwise without prior written permission of the author/publisher, except as provided by United States copyright law.

All Scripture quotations are from the New International Version of the Bible.

This book was printed in the United States of America.

First Edition 2010

To order additional copies of this book, contact:
Xlibris Corporation
1-888-795-4274
www.Xlibris.com
Orders@Xlibris.com

CONTENTS

Chapter 1: European Vacation 11

Chapter 2: Love of my life 21

Chapter 3: Marriage Sanctified by the Holy Spirit 33

Chapter 4: Near Death Experience 35

Chapter 5: Bed & Breakfast 40

Chapter 6: Whitewater Rafting 47

Chapter 7: National TV Appearances 59

Chapter 8: Travels to Every City in America 69

Chapter 9: Million Dollar Deal by Noon 87

Chapter 10: Blessings Beyond Belief 91

Chapter 11: Satan at My Front Door 102

Chapter 12: The Turning Point—Divorce 115

Chapter 13: High Roller in Vegas 125

Chapter 14: Rehab 143

Chapter 15: Visions from the Holy Spirit 147

Chapter 16: Wickedness Beyond Comprehension 151

Chapter 17: Imprisoned 161

Chapter 18: Morning Star Rises in Your Heart 173

Chapter 19: Higher Power 178

Chapter 20: The Power of the Lord; "Justice" 182

Chapter 21: God's Will Always Prevails 188

Chapter 22: When the Truth is Unbelievable 195

Chapter 23: One Breath Away from Eternity 200

Chapter 24: Destiny; Mountains are Moved and Things Happen at Lightning Speed 207

Chapter 25: Leave no One Behind 212

Dedication

This book is dedicated to everyone I've met during my travels in life, with the hope that I have touched their lives or made a difference in their journey as well.

To my daughters, Paris and Skyler; words could never express my love for my girls. The two of you have brought more joy into my life than I could ever imagine. There is no greater love than what a dad has for his daughters. To Haley; you were a blessing to our family.

To my mom, and family, with the hope that their lives have been touched in some way, and a difference made in their journey as well.

To the other friends I've met who have encouraged me, or made a difference in my life throughout my journey, especially Pastor Linda and Cynthia.

To you who read this book, may this be a blessing on your journey.

-Kyle L. Coon

INTRODUCTION

"You have to have faith, even against seemingly insurmountable odds."

An insightful, life-changing read is all set to inspire and help anyone who takes the right path towards their ultimate goal in life. *'What I Learned Under the Sun',* is a unique memoir that relates the author's journey in life, love, and marriage. He also reveals the wonderful lessons he learned to help anyone make the best out of their lives.

This book will inspire readers to learn to understand the basic realities of life, how to make the right decisions, how to have faith, to be able to face and triumph against seemingly insurmountable odds.

'What I Learned Under the Sun', is my life story of blessings, that anyone can do whatever they want in life if one has faith, and all their dreams will come true.

The book is packed with adventures in life, traveling the world, having been blessed, and having blessed many people along my journey. You can be overwhelmed with blessings, on top of blessings, but when one turns from God in a marriage, and when you make wrong decisions in life, disasters follow.

'What I Learned Under the Sun', will inspire people looking for hope. That no matter how bad things seem, if you keep the faith, all the right doors will open up for you.

We go through life with blinders on as we chase after the wind. We look for love in all the wrong places, dodging obstacles, and disappointment after disappointment. And still, we don't get it. It took me awhile to figure out that life is short, and the secret to any man's success is having a good woman behind him—the key is in your heart.

When you figure that out and turn from sin; all the right doors will open and the Lord will guide you down the right path. In that moment in time, you will be on the right path to your predetermined destiny and only then will all your dreams come true.

You must live by faith, even against seemingly insurmountable odds, and you will be blessed beyond your wildest dreams.

A journey of love sanctified by the Holy Spirit can still turn to deception, adultery, evil, and wickedness beyond comprehension, yet end in a true Cinderella story that could only be influenced by a Higher Power.

No matter how bad it gets, you have to have faith, believe that God's Will, will always prevail and everything works out in the end. True love is a lifelong process of commitment, sacrifice, and enduring hardships. We're all searching for perfect love filled with passion and romance. And in the end, you'll find that the answer is within your reach . . . if you open your heart to find it.

Many couple's stories are the same—just different characters, place and time. We all have trials and tribulations, yet we are conquerors, no matter what you may be facing this day, know this . . . . through your faith, you come out on top—always.

Marriage will either give you rest or restlessness. The choice is yours. It all depends on what you want, the thoughts you think, and who you listen to. We're all blessed with FREE will. *'What I've Learned Under the Sun'*, is life isn't always fair, you better believe that you will reap what you sow, and the most important thing is, keeping the faith; no matter how bad things seem. God will open all the right doors for you and you will find your destiny under the sun!

Chapter One

EUROPEAN VACATION

You're here today. Like a speeding bullet, thirty years have passed you by. All of those years, where did they go, what did you do, why are you here? What happened? And have you made the right decisions in your life?

My journey under the sun can be summed up by; "My Unbelievable Life . . . when the Truth is Unbelievable!" Describing Kyle would be hard, girls that had crushes on him would probably say "wild", very wild, a man living on the edge with no fear, that would never see his fortieth birthday.

Just out of high school and fortunate enough to land a factory job, my brain still raced on what I wanted in life. I wanted to know my destiny, and how to get there. But I had no clue what I wanted to do. Like every other kid, I wanted to fish professionally, invent something, make a million dollars, or travel the world looking for adventure, but not knowing how to get started.

Maybe I was shy, but I didn't have time for girls to slow me down. They were fun to hang out with at all the school parties and the beach, but I got nervous when they sought a close relationship.

My neighbor's had a niece, Irene, who visited them often in the summers. I hung out with Irene for a few weeks, then she went back home to Denver, Colorado. Just as fast as she came into my life she went out of it. We had a lot of fun together and developed a long distance relationship. I even flew out to Denver, to visit with her and her parents. Over-time, however, we drifted apart when I started working in a factory called Howmet, making predominantly aircraft blades for jet engines.

When I started at Howmet, another girl came into my life. I opened my heart, as she captivated me, and within a week we lived together at her place or mine. What we did wasn't good. We allowed sin to enter our relationship. In fact, most of our relationship was built on sin. And listen, it doesn't matter who you love, when sin takes a foothold it destroys any relationship. Look at today's statistics. Our divorce rate is at a staggering fifty percent—wow! They give out divorces like speeding tickets. Then everyone races to their next victim.

The cycle never ends. Trying to find the love of your life? I know you see beauty in her like you've never seen before. She is slim, athletic with curves in the right places, and topped with a beautiful, angelic face. She takes your breath away. You both thought it was love. But really it was passionate lust for each other that eventually blossomed into love.

In my life, this beauty's name was Brenda. We fell more in love every day, but seemed to forget each other when we went to parties. I forgot about her, or left her in the background much more than she did me. I didn't want the commitment of a relationship. I didn't mean to let that pretty new girl at work seduce me, and pick me up at the bar. Maybe it was the Lion in me, but I was hard to tame, and living a life of sin. I didn't have a care in the world. Not even for my own soul.

One night Brenda went out to a local bar. I took off all the blankets on the bed, then dumped a whole box of cereal underneath, then remade the bed. I figured if Brenda brought a guy home, they'd have quite a surprise when they jumped in the sack. Like the angel she was, she came home alone. But she told me that she laughed her butt off when she got into bed that night.

Brenda tried to tame me many times, but the only attempt that came remotely close was her daughter, Rita. I'll never forget the first time I held Rita, or the first time she held out her hands and softly whispered, "Daddy."

The moment I held her in my arms and looked into her eyes, love came over me like I've never felt before. I felt as though she were my own child. She became the love of my life and meant everything to me. She brought more joy into my life than I could ever put into words.

At that point in life, I only cared about the good times, a need for speed, living on the edge with no fear. But Brenda and I, along with Rita, had a lot of memorable times. I loved being around Brenda's family.

Deer hunting or camping—her entire family embodied fun. I became very fond of her entire family, her parents, and their friends.

Growing up in Michigan, it seemed like everyone hunted deer. It was like a national Holiday. Kids even get the day off from school.

One Thanksgiving Brenda and I were at her grandma's house.

"I'm going out back to chase a deer," I said to Brenda, and she followed me outside.

A cold breeze filled the air that morning. The ground, partially covered in snow, crunched under our feet as we walked down an old road to the edge of the swamp thicket. We passed a small clearing with a bunch of cedar trees.

"Stand here, I'm going to walk around the swamp thicket and chase the deer in your direction. Don't shoot me," I told Brenda. "Shoot the deer when he comes around."

I made my way to the other side. I was about two feet into the thicket when I heard a sound. I looked back. A deer took off toward Brenda. A gunshot fired through the air, rustling the thicket. The deer almost ran over her, but she managed to knock it down with one shot. I think she tried to put her gloves on so she wouldn't break a nail, or maybe she was taking the gloves off to shoot me, and then by sheer luck hit the deer.

Either way, I was so happy for her. By now, the snow began to melt, and I could only find a few deer hairs on the ground. Brenda must have shot him in the tail or just plain scared the crap out of him, but I never found it. I bet today she wished she had shot me. It would have been called an "Accidental Homicide." *I thought my boyfriend was a deer!*

Another time my friend Jimbo, and I went raccoon hunting. The wind chilled my face and the fog was barely visible a few feet above the ground in the full moonlight. We were knee-deep in the middle of the swamp. I wore a black leather coat and from all the sharp briers, I had a lot of dried blood on my face. Nearly an hour before sunrise, we decided to try one more spot.

Our dogs treed some raccoons in the middle of a Christmas tree plantation in an old hollow tree. I stuck my hand in the tree to shoot the raccoons and hit a porcupine. It fell on my hand, and stuck me with a bunch of quills. As I pulled them out, a horn blasted on the two-track we were parked on. I figured someone showed up to harvest Christmas trees and needed us to move our truck.

When I pulled the quills out of my hand blood went everywhere. I ran through the pines towards the horn, I was very close to them, almost on top of them when the horn blasted again.

My face had dried blood on it from the briers; my hand was bleeding from the darn porcupine.

As I popped out of the Christmas trees, six migrant workers stood around a truck complaining.

I said, "What's your problem?"

They turned, looked at me, and their mouths dropped open, they all ran to their truck, jumped in and took off so fast they pummeled over some Christmas trees.

Barely having control of their vehicle. *"What the heck is their problem?"* I thought.

A few seconds later, I pulled out a cigarette, when I went to light it, I saw blood. *"I must've scared the crap out of them,"* I thought.

When I got home, Brenda said, "What happened to you last night?"

"It was a tough night coon hunting." I replied.

I walked into the bathroom, looked into the mirror, and about died.

I thought about the migrant workers. They must've thought I murdered someone based on the way I looked. I wonder if they ever came back. Or maybe the poor farmer had to hire a new crew to harvest Christmas trees.

What a weekend, back to reality ~ work!

I became restless at work, doing the same thing, day in and day out. I would rather be hunting or fishing. Working in a factory nine-to-five wasn't my calling in life. There had to be more out there. I had no clue, though. So, I searched for anything I could think of and thought maybe I'd do something related to fishing, since I loved it so much.

"They" say if you do something you enjoy you'll be happy in life. In the past, I fished for salmon and steelhead a lot, when they were spawning. After I caught a fish, I was using river rocks or sticks to prevent lost eggs, saving the eggs for future use as bait.

I invented a plastic device called the "Spawn Saver" with a cap on the end to milk the eggs out. I spent a lot of hours developing the Spawn Saver, making prototypes, and I even had an engineering firm design it for my patent application process.

I educated myself on what to do and how to get it to the market. Rita spent a lot of time working with me at the kitchen table. She colored in her books, while I did sales and marketing research. It seemed to bring us very close together. It took a few years to get everything together, but the final product looked awesome, and the packaging was very attractive.

The packaging was a blister card and had two Spawn Savers, in a clear plastic holder that was heat sealed onto the card itself. The graphics was a picture of a salmon showing a cut-away of the insides of a fish showing the eggs. It showed the Spawn Saver in use coming out of the fish with an open cap and with eggs flowing out and down the front of the packaging.

Ironically it was a blue background, the graphics color was the same as this book, not a color I would have picked out or liked. But then I'm not a graphics artist.

Not familiar with funding, I had a friend line up some investors for the Spawn Saver business venture. In the end, he did a wild takeover, and somehow managed to own fifty-one-percent of the company. He then ousted me when I was in Europe. Since I did all the work, they thought they could they take it over and sell the product themselves.

One thing they didn't count on was my relationship with the buyers in the sporting goods industry, who were my personal friends. After what the investors did to me, none of the sporting goods buyers would have anything to do with them.

The business took me deeper with other companies. Throughout the contacts, I ended up with ice-fishing products. Those same products somehow got me involved with fishing in 1991 in the world ice fishing championships in Sweden.

Who would have thought that would happen? Not me. What a ride! It started out in Atlanta, Georgia, and took us to Stockholm, Sweden.

The plane to Sweden took off in the evening.

As we crossed over Newfoundland, I looked out the window, and could see the "aurora borealis" dancing across the night sky. It took my breath away. The beautiful show out of my window seemed to go on forever. A pillow cradled my head, as my thoughts drifted to how much I missed Brenda and Rita.

This was my first of seven trips out of the country and I was nervous. We spent two nights in Stockholm. Our hotel room was beyond spectacular. Walking through the city didn't compare to what I'd seen, except some displays on television. My eyes saw a whole new world.

In the hallway of the hotel room there was a huge king's chair. I sat there for two hours, thinking about life, and what my family was up to.

I had an early wake-up call, to head to the airport, where we would leave for Amsterdam, then onto Lovanger, Sweden, for the tournament. At Amsterdam, the amount of armed guards around amazed me. You didn't see that stateside in the mid-eighties. We found our terminal in the Amsterdam airport and then boarded our flight.

We went from nice weather and emerald green grass, back to a snow-covered runway. After departing the plane and going through customs, we took a short trip by van to the site. As strange as it was . . . our cabins were small, with bunk beds and everything was crafted with handmade wood furniture. They had a lot of cabins with anglers from USA, Russia, Sweden, Iceland, Finland, and Canada.

The culture was a lot different than what I had been familiar with. Men and women used the same rest rooms. We ate fish for breakfast; I guess reindeer—or was it a moose?—for dinner every day.

The dinner hall had a snowed-in circular drive with a water fountain in the center. At the entrance, six steps went down into two large doors.

One day while I was there, I sat with a Canadian pal on top of a hill in town. He sat on something that seemed like a bike, but had a ski on the front. He urged me to sit on the handlebars to slide down the long hill to the dinner hall.

As we went down our speed increased so fast that he couldn't make the turn and crashed into the snow bank. I went airborne over the water fountain, cleared it, did a flip in mid air, and landed on the other side in the driveway on my feet. I took two big steps and stood next to some Russians standing at the door.

They looked at me and said, "Rambo".

How I did that . . . I have no clue. But it was way too cool. Ever since that moment the Russians and I got along great. At the end of the tournament they were taking team pictures and the Russians wanted me in their photograph. It was a trip to remember, that's for sure.

As I boarded the plane to Amsterdam, my new Russian friends were on my flight. One of them yelled, "Hey Rambo, you want some Vodka?"

Our last night was a big party. I drank way too much Vodka with them in their cabins. I invited them over to my cabin. They brought me Russian Souvenirs. They liked my "Levi Jeans" so I gave them everything I had in my suitcase.

On the plane, they hugged me, and then thanked me again.

It makes me feel good inside to do something for someone when they appreciated it more than I'd ever know.

When we got into Amsterdam, our group loaded up in vans and went to a hotel by the airport for two nights to tour the town. After lunch, everyone went on a planned tour and I decided to do my own thing—imagine that!

A train outside my hotel welcomed passengers, and I thought *"what the heck? Let's see where it goes."* No one on the train spoke English, so I got off when everyone else did.

I ended up downtown in the center district of Amsterdam. Talk about colorful! I found my way to a bar. Would you believe the bartender actually spoke English? I stayed there for a few hours until the bartender was about to get off. She wanted to know if I wanted to go with her and her friend to see the sights.

We met a friend of hers at another bar. They were talking in Dutch, giggling often.

We walked around what seemed like the whole city. Dragging me here and there, they held onto my arms as we walked down the street laughing.

The night began to slip into morning when they decided to walk me to the station and help me find the right train to my hotel. On the way, we passed—of all things—a Pizza Hut. So we ate there before I left.

Only one girl spoke English. At the train she told me her friend liked me a lot, and wanted to go with me. I told her I had an early flight, gave them both a hug, and then I boarded the train. She jumped on the train. I turned around; she kissed and hugged me again.

Wow, I thought. I didn't see that coming. As the train sped away, the girls waved goodbye to me. Twenty minutes later I arrived at the Hotel. Some of the guys were in the lobby. A few of them hustled over to me, one of them said, *"Where in the heck have you been?"*

I smiled, *"sight-seeing."* The trip ended so fast, I thought, as I reclined on a KLM flight to the States. Brenda told me she was nervous about my flight while she waited at Detroit Metropolitan International Airport. Then, a random guy walked up to her and said, *"Don't be nervous, everything will be okay. He'll make it home."* Looking back, I wonder if that guy was an angel trying to comfort her.

I can't tell you how many times throughout my twenties I should have died, but by the grace of God my life was spared. In our lives we all have angels to protect and comfort us. Most of the time we don't even realize it but, we as humans sure do make them laugh.

They intervene in our lives, and we never see them. We never even knew we had a need for protection. I'm talking about close calls and nearly dying in accidents. It's the times you never knew about that the Lord was watching over you to carry out His purpose for your life.

When I got off the plane from Amsterdam, Brenda smiled the most beautiful smile I've ever seen. So happy to be in her arms again, I didn't realize it would be one of the last times we'd ever be together.

Shortly after returning from Europe, my so-called partners kicked me out of the company, and took it over. This strained Brenda and me monetarily, mentally, and physically. The stress took a toll on our relationship which ended without question soon after.

Chapter Two

LOVE OF MY LIFE

I will never forget the day when Brenda and I broke up. It shattered my heart even after all the times I cheated on her, as though I just lost the "Love of my life". It broke me, but it had to end. I walked down to the lake, sat on the dock, staring into the water and thinking about our life together. What went wrong? What could I have done different? Why did this have to happen?

Now, wisdom tells me that everything happens for reason. We're on God's time and He has a plan for us. We have to learn to take the good with the bad, even when doors are closing all around us.

Back then, I didn't know where I went wrong, but I finally figured it out after many, many years. I lived a party lifestyle and if you live a life of sin you will never find true happiness—sooner or later it will all catch up to you.

Anyone that knew me at Howmet might have thought I was a little crazy then again maybe not! I did hang out way too much with Jimbo whom always got me in trouble when we went out or did I get him in trouble. I think the only time I didn't get into any trouble was riding Harley's with my friend Dave.

I also probably spent way too much time at Bob's house, my other friend whom I worked with in the gauging department at Howmet. One day I was leaving Bob's house headed to work, I was backing out of his driveway onto Roosevelt road. I stopped for traffic and had this feeling that I learned a lesson today called; wisdom, that one day I will pass onto my kids.

I would describe Bob as worldly old school money, when I think of Bob I think of "Rothschild's" or a mysterious man, yet very intriguing. The man was a world of knowledge when it came to antiques, antiquities, and world history. I probably learned more from Bob than my entire twelve years in school, but then again we hung out for ten years before I quit Howmet, and moved to Alabama.

You can call it whatever. If I wouldn't have been so selfish, spent a lot less time away, allowing Jimbo and Bob to get me into trouble on the weekends, more time would have been spent with Brenda and Rita, I'm sure our relationship would have been a lot closer.

I loved Brenda and Rita, but never truly gave them my heart. If I had given Brenda my heart, we probably would have moved mountains together.

I lived the party lifestyle and never proposed to her. If I truly loved her, I would have married her, and adopted her daughter. I would have given up the party lifestyle. Would have we had a great life together? Absolutely, if I would have changed my ways, turned to the Lord, showed her respect, and learned to be sensitive to her needs.

Thank God she now has a great husband. I'm thankful for that. She is a very special girl, and deserves the best life has to offer. To this day, she still hasn't aged a bit after sixteen years.

She's still slim, attractive, and has a million dollar smile that glows. I'll always be proud of her when I hear good things about her. It is a small world we live in, but it's always a good feeling when you hear good news about someone you loved.

The pain of the break up was more than I could bear, but I still had no sense of direction of where I was headed. So I kept on my destructive path at high speed, bored-to-death as I worked at Howmet.

One night I stopped at a bar and ran into an old friend from school. She was having problems in her marriage. We sat at the end of the bar talking as we watched Monday Night Football. When the game ended, I drove her home; we sat in her driveway talking for what felt like hours. I finally convinced her to try and work out her marriage problems.

Ironically, she became friends with a new guy where she worked, then started having an affair with him. I spent most of the night trying to convince her that it wasn't love at all, but lust of the flesh—the number one killer of any marriage.

Her husband never knew about the affair. I saw her in a store years later, she thanked me, told me they were still married today because of what I said that night in her driveway.

She never knew that night when I left her house; a cop pulled me over, arrested me for an OUI, and took me to jail. In jail, I was peeved, because I could have spent the night with her, but decided that wasn't the right thing to do after talking her out of having an affair.

I had a fishing buddy who was a lawyer. He got me off with a fine to pay and had the charge dropped to impaired driving. It had been months since the breakup, but I still couldn't get Brenda out of my mind. I missed love in my life and desperately wanted to find a special someone to fill that void in my heart to ease the pain.

My cousin told me that an old friend named Marlene was single again. She urged me to give her a call. I thought, *"cool, haven't seen her in like ten years."* I called Marlene and her mother answered the phone.

There was a long hesitation before Marlene spoke, when she did, she said, *"Well, there is only one Kyle."*

That began a sixteen-year relationship. She had a son named Eric, and we made plans to take him to a party that afternoon. I picked them up.

We went to a mutual friend's house, "The Beatties", in Holton, Michigan. Being a very small town, everyone knew us, and was betting whether we would end up together after the party.

We got a little carried away late in the morning, made out in a chair in the garage and broke it. Late in the morning we decided to go to her house, which led us to stay up until after the sun came up. Marlene was a party girl, so we went out constantly to dance and have fun.

I remained friends with Brenda and Rita though, and made plans to take Rita up north to a meeting I had with a new company that wanted me to handle their line. So I picked Rita up and the four of us Marlene, Eric, Rita, and I went up north. It felt weird, and that's an understatement. Rita didn't like me being with another woman. She stayed by her dad's side the entire time, I loved it.

My meeting took place in Marquette, Michigan. We vacationed there a few days. I took everyone to Lake Superior where huge cliffs surrounded the lake. As we made our way down the trail we stopped and stood on the front of the cliff. I told Marlene that I would be right back and walked out to the end of the cliff.

A young couple lay on the rocks talking. I walked over to the edge, looked down into Lake Superior, stepped back, and stripped my clothes off to my underwear. The couple looked at me like I lost my mind.

Marlene yelled from shore, *"Don't do it!"*

Without a doubt, she knew I'd jump.

I didn't realize how far down it was until I hit the water. Talk about cold—wow! I climbed back up the cliff, they all ran out to find me, but couldn't see me in the water until my hand came up over the ledge.

Marlene said, *"Don't ever do that again."*

"What?"

I climbed up, got dressed and we walked back off the rocks and headed to the van. Next, we went to a park that had tame deer. Rita loved petting them. I had a picture taken of us with a big six-point buck, with me holding Rita as she petted the deer's back.

After leaving Marquette we stayed in Mackinac City (Mackinaw City). I took everyone on a train ride to see the Tahquamenon Falls. Rita sat with me, Marlene sat with Eric. Having not seen me for some time, Rita enjoyed every minute of the trip and held my hand the whole time on the train. On that vacation I was truly feeling love, more than I have before in my life. And I loved every minute with Rita; I truly missed watching her grow up.

Marlene hated it because she wanted nothing to do with Rita, and wanted me to give all my attention to her son, which I thought was selfish on her part.

When I dropped Rita off at Brenda's, tears flowed endlessly down my face. I felt like I'd never see her again.

Later, Marlene actually gave me an ultimatum, her or Rita, making me choose between her, a woman that I wanted to have in my life, and a child whom I have grown to love and care for. If I called Rita or Brenda ever again she would leave me. Brenda had another man and Marlene had been in my life for a few months now.

Daily, she pounded in my brain, "Rita's not your kid. You're not part of that family anymore."

But in my heart Rita was my daughter and always would be. No one could ever take away love in your heart for someone. The pressure to never speak to her broke my heart. So, to have the best of both worlds, I called Rita when Marlene wasn't around.

When the phone bill came, let's just say Marlene wasn't happy. It ticked her off so much that she went out partying.

The bar closed and she never came home. I started to wonder if she got into an accident with her friend. Finally, around 4:00 am she came home.

"My friend wouldn't give me a ride home," she said. "Some guy at the bar drugged me, and then took me to his house. I slept on the couch, but nothing happened."

In my mind it bothered me that I'd question her faithfulness so soon, but when I asked her about it she ate her breakfast, wiped her mouth, and said, "I've done no wrong." She blamed the guy who "drugged her."

On top of that, not being allowed to see Rita on her ninth birthday bothered the heck out of me. Some things you never forget. I'm writing this book eighteen years later. Rita's now twenty-seven and I still think of her. Today is February 24th; Rita's mother's birthday was two days ago on the 22nd. Over time some things you just never forget, that's the beauty of love within all of us. No matter what, you're going to always remember special dates you've shared together.

'*What I learned Under the Sun*', is people come into your life, leave a lot of happy memories that last forever. The bad memories filter out over time through forgiveness, for most people, if you truly loved them. To this day I never had a bad thought about Brenda, but only fond memories we had together in our life.

It's hard to forgive in the moment of time, but I had to swallow my pride, believe Marlene, and what she said about being drugged.

A few weeks later, I had to go back up to Marquette on a business trip and Marlene brought a girlfriend of hers named "Sherry". We stayed at a cabin in the woods. It was pretty awesome, secluded on a private lake, owned by a millionaire friend of mine.

There was a winding trail that took awhile to find because it was very secluded. It was built within the natural surroundings of the area; you couldn't see the cabin until you were at the front door.

The property was loaded with wildlife and the cabin had huge pine logs it was built out of and was two stories high.

The cabin had a huge fireplace, on each side there were very large picture windows that overlooked the private lake. It was spectacular watching two loons swim across the lake.

The guy I had a meeting with stayed with us. All weekend he kept telling us to be quieter. We were too loud for him. I thought to myself, we're in the middle of the woods on what seems like miles of private land on vacation for the weekend. Why do we have to be so quiet? "So we don't scare the squirrels?"

When we left the cabin to go home, I had a brick of firecrackers in the car from the fourth of July. He said goodbye from the window. I reached down, lit the brick, and then tossed them outside the window, so I could leave him with a bang, making a lot of noise. Well, luck has it; the firecrackers hit the window, I didn't have it all the way down and the brick fell back into the car.

It happened so fast the three of us couldn't get out of the car. We covered our heads and I laughed as the girls screamed their heads off. After the noise quit, we all jumped out of the car laughing as the smoke billowed out the doors.

On our drive back going over the Mackinac Bridge I think there was still smoke coming out of the car; it took another four hours to get home before I think it finally started to clear up. It took me a week to clean the car after we got home, months for the smell of gunpowder to get out of the car.

The following weekend Sherry wanted Marlene and me to go to a party in town about an hour away from our home. It was with a bunch of her other friends.

"*Sure,*" I said. "*But we're going to stay in town. I'm not driving home that late at night.*"

We stopped at a few bars on the way and it was late when we got to the house party. I was more interested in leaving so we could go to the motel but Marlene was having too much fun, and wanted to stay later.

We left the party about 1:00 am. When we got to the car I told Marlene; I have a big surprise for you. *"But you have to put on a blindfold and promise not to take it off."*

About three miles down the road, I planned to turn into the parking lot of a hotel. As I got off the exit ramp a cop pulled me over.

Marlene said, excitedly "Are we here?" Then I said, *"Not yet. I have to pull over for a second. Don't take off your blindfold!"*

A cop walked up to the window and said, "Ma'am, are you all right"? She took the blindfold off and said; "Oh, yeah, I'm fine."

She didn't listen very well. I told her not to take off the blindfold. The cop called another car and took me to jail for being impaired. He took Marlene to the motel and left the car on the side of the road.

She waited at the motel until the cops left, and then walked a mile down the freeway to our car. Then she drove an hour home, got some money, and came back to bail me out. My lawyer dragged it out in court for months. I refused to drive anymore, Marlene didn't want to so, we stopped going out.

That was the best move the both of us did in a long time.

By this time I had worked at Howmet for ten years. Brenda still worked there, with all the tension at home, Marlene wanted me out of there, so she convinced me to quit. She then told me we should move down south where she once lived to start our new life together.

I said, "What are we going to do? Where are we going to live?"

She said, "Don't worry. The Lord will provide for us."

I never saw that side of her before then. After that she opened up to me about another side of her I never knew, talking about all the hard times with her ex-boyfriend, when they traveled flat broke, God always provided for them.

I was convinced. So I decided to work one more day, and give them my two weeks' notice. On the way to work driving down the expressway, I saw a cloud formation in the sky that looked like a perfect 2989, there wasn't any other clouds in the sky. When I got to work I told my supervisor, she said, "I saw the same thing driving into work, so I stopped at the gas station and played them in the daily lottery."

At work I told everyone the news, someone said, "You can't do that, you have ten years in here. This is your life, you can't give that up". As I was walking out the door my supervisor said, "Those numbers came out in the daily lottery, and she won! Now that's a sign."

I had no idea what awaited me, but I wanted to find out if there was more to life. The next day after I quit Howmet, I told my lawyer friend I was leaving town, and blowing off my court date. "Yeah, wow." That was my lawyer's thoughts, too; *"Yeah. Are you crazy? Only Kyle would do that."*

Marlene and I went to Huntsville, Alabama; it became my responsibility to find a job, and a place to live.

I found a guy in the mountains outside of Huntsville, who wanted a marketing person to run his hunting resort booking hunting trips. That sounded like fun and seemed to be in my line of work. It didn't take long for me to get the job.

So Marlene went back up to Hesperia, Michigan, to pack her stuff, and get Eric who was staying at the grandparent's house while we went to Alabama. A few weeks later, Marlene and Eric arrived, and I had second thoughts about working for this guy named Jerry.

I have to admit, the few weeks I was there seemed eerie. This guy, in his late seventies, was always talking on the phone in German. I never figured it out, but had a feeling he was hiding in those mountains in Alabama for a reason.

I was working like crazy, almost like a slave, having all I could do handling this old guy named Jerry. So before Marlene and Eric got down there, I found us another place to stay a few blocks away.

Marlene and Eric were going to arrive today and that made me very happy. I spent hours at the end of the drive, on this long curvy road in the Mountains of Alabama waiting to see them.

When I saw the car come around the corner, I don't think I was ever so happy in my life. Marlene pulled in, parked the car, got out, kissed me, and then said, *"You look like Cool Hand Luke!"*

I told her, I was working hard, and it showed. I jumped in the car and took her to the cabin we were staying in. Eric slept in the car and hadn't awaked yet, so I carried him into the cabin, tucking him into bed. Then Marlene and I went to bed. I had this feeling the next morning; I thought for sure she was pregnant.

We didn't even unpack the car, and after Eric woke up, we moved into another house. I had no luck finding another job right away, so I was going to apply for a bouncer position at a bar in Huntsville.

The neighbor we rented the house from, watched Eric while we went into town to apply for that job. We got to the bar, walked in, and met the owner at the door, he said, "Have you ever had any experience getting into a bar fight?"

Marlene laughed and said; "Oh, yeah, he has tons of experience getting into bar fights."

It was around seven at night, the owner laughed, and said, "You look pretty tough." I'll tell you what, "if you can go to the Silver Dollar Saloon in Huntsville, and come out alive, then come back. You'll have the job."

We left and I thought about it. We rode by the saloon and checked it out first. It was a little bar in a strip mall. We went down the road to another bar and had a few drinks.

Then I said to Marlene, *"Let's do this."*

She said, "No, way."

And off to the Silver Dollar Saloon we went. I opened the door for her, we walked in, went to the empty bar, and ordered two drinks. Two bikers sat near the dance floor where an awesome band was playing.

I walked over to their table and grabbed one of their chairs. Then, I took Marlene out on the dance floor, sat her in the chair, giving her a lap dance.

I didn't pay attention to the bikers, but they disappeared at some point. We stayed on the dance floor dancing what seemed like an hour, just the two of us being alone (except for the band), and the bar maid. The band announced they would be right back and took a break.

Marlene and I turned around. The lights came on in a side room filled with smoke. Both our jaws dropped. Fifty or sixty of the biggest, meanest looking ZZ Top bikers I had ever seen in my life we're sitting there staring at us.

I said, "To heck with this, we're out of here."

I grabbed our leather coats off the table, and then went to pay the tab.

The bartender said, "You two aren't going anywhere. Here is a drink on the house. You're too much fun to watch, everyone wants you to stay here."

We looked at each other, smiled and started laughing, thinking, "*If I could make it out alive,* Right."

We danced a few more sets, and left, never went back to the other bar for the job. That's the thing about the two of us, no matter where we went, we usually were the life of the party. I don't think you could put two people together with more similar personalities then us.

About a month went by and Marlene said to me, "I think, I'm pregnant." I had a feeling that was coming but was still shocked, waited a minute, and then said, "Are you sure?"

Marlene said; "No, but I have a pregnancy test, we can find out."

She handed me the bag. I pulled it out and froze. We stared at each other a few minutes.

Finally, I said, "Well, let's see".

She followed the directions. We stood together hand and hand, patiently waited to see what color it turned, positive. We were going to have a baby!

I hugged her, and said, *"I love you. Everything will work out. Will you marry me before the baby is born?"*

She said, "Yes."

Later, we made arrangements to fly to Las Vegas and get married. It's not like we just decided to get married and that was it.

Marlene already had chosen a beautiful white dress and had a big wedding planned back in Michigan. I got cold feet, from having second thoughts about marrying her.

Chapter Three

MARRIAGE SANCTIFIED BY THE HOLY SPIRIT

We decided on September 3rd, 1993, but I still had cold feet so we got married on the 5th. My hesitation was biblical. I believed if two people were joined together, they became one, and that you stay married forever. I only wanted one wife in my life; I knew I was making a covenant with God until death would part us. I just wanted to be sure I married the right woman.

As we prepared for our wedding, I enjoyed watching my future wife transform herself into a beautiful angel. We were staying at the Imperial Palace, and decided to get married at their Chapel called "We've Only Just Begun Wedding Chapel."

When we walked into the chapel, an overwhelming sense of peace that I've never felt before came over me. We were alone, minus the female pastor that married us. Marlene and I looked into each other's eyes, and then tears flowed down both of our cheeks. We were crying so hard the pastor started to cry during the ceremony.

At that moment I felt true love in my heart for my wife. I could feel the Holy Spirit working in us as we held hands, gazing into each other's eyes. What an overwhelming sense of joy. Tears still flowed from my eyes as we said our vows.

The pastor could hardly pronounce us man and wife because she was crying so hard. She said it was the only wedding she'd ever done, and felt the presence of God. The Holy Spirit sanctified our marriage, even though we were living in sin up to this day. When we left I felt God truly had a purpose for us. It was Him who brought us together in the first place through some major turn of events.

I think we were both numb for the better part of the day. We kept a list of all the wild things that happened while getting married in Las Vegas. Like riding in a limo to the city hall with another couple that just got married, she was in a leopard outfit.

The week literally flew by in Las Vegas. We were exhausted when we boarded the plane. We hit our seats, collapsing in each other's arms.

Not quite as adventurous as the flight when we both locked ourselves in the bathroom for an hour. When we walked out everyone on the plane clapped. We missed dinner, but the stewardess gave us wings for joining the mile high club.

Anyway, our wedding was my most memorable week ever. We came home with some very colorful souvenirs from our wedding.

Our wedding happiness ignited deep in my heart, I knew God had big plans for our future. I had an overwhelming sensation that our family would be very, very blessed.

Even before the wedding, I saw beautiful talents my wife possessed and couldn't wait for her to use them. She was a gifted artist. She painted a picture one day of the dunes by Lake Michigan where we spent time. It was an absolutely breathtaking painting. I thought to myself, one day I'm going to get my wife a studio where she can do her painting and sell them.

I missed Eric being away from him so long, and I loved being with him back home. Over the next seven months Marlene grew bigger, and sexier in my eyes. I never got a break on a job, but found some construction work to get us by.

Not too long after, Marlene talked about moving to West Virginia, to try our luck there. Eric's dad lived there. I didn't like the idea too much, having her ex-boyfriend involved in our lives. So I said, "Give me a few weeks to think about it."

Chapter Four

NEAR DEATH EXPERIENCE

A few weeks passed. I told Marlene to give her ex-boyfriend a call, we'd move to West Virginia, so Eric could be closer to his father. I was going to run down the road to a guy's house I worked with, who had a card game going on, and let them know we were moving.

The Alabama roads in the mountains were very small, had many curves and I think I only had like two miles to go. When I got there they were playing cards in the garage, I hung out for a few hours before I decided to head back home.

When I left it was pitch black out that night, as I was heading home, I tried to light a cigarette just down the road. Then I dropped the cigarette, when I reached down, I had a vision that someone grabbed my arm, and pulled me out of my seat. The next thing I remember was my wife saying, *"Get up, Kyle. Please. You're not dead"*.

Marlene told me the next day, that she walked next door to the neighbor's house, when the phone rang. Marlene answered it, and the caller said, "Get your neighbor lady. Her husband just hit the tree in our yard, and he died." Marlene freaked out, got a ride from the old man named Howard to the accident. Marlene said, when she turned the corner she saw the dark night sky lit up by flashers.

Being pregnant, just married, I can't imagine what went through Marlene's mind when she turned the corner, thinking her husband just died. Marlene told me she ran up to the van, where the police and the first responders tried to restrain her.

My wife didn't accept that, broke loose from her coat, and ran to the back windows of the van that were shattered from the impact.

I was in a fetal position, my face covered in blood. Marlene yelled at me, *"Get up, Kyle; please, you're not dead."*

The first responders were trying to pull her away from the van, she said that I kicked open the door and stepped out of the van. Everyone stood there, shocked. The police and the first responders shined their flashlights on me, after declaring me dead.

Still in a daze, I didn't realize I was in an accident. Marlene said she grabbed someone's light, looked over my body from head-to-toe. When she got to my boots, she saw blood bubbling out.

Everyone was screaming for me to lie down.

"I'm fine," I said, then walked over to the porch near the house and sat down.

Marlene lifted up my pant leg, she could see through the flesh in my calf right to the bone. Marlene wrapped my leg in a towel as the ambulance showed up.

I guess they weren't in a hurry since they thought I was dead. At the hospital they stitched me up, and kept me overnight for observation.

Marlene took me home, helped me into bed, which took some time. My body ached and I could hardly walk.

A few days later Marlene called her ex-boyfriend to see if he could find a car, and bring it down to us. When I got up to move around, I went outside to look at the van. The damage shocked me. That's when Marlene told me what happened.

I looked at the driver's seat. If I would've been sitting in it, I would have been dead. Two people prior to my accident died hitting the same tree. The steering column on the van was completely crushed into the seat.

I remembered, a hand pull me out right before the impact. That had to be one of the only times I didn't wear my seatbelt. Dried blood covered the back of the van. Marlene told me the jack went through my leg and severed my calf to the bone. Today it resembles a shark bite.

After the accident I realized that my wife willed me back to life that night. We truly became one in spirit.

I never told anyone about the hand. Was it God Himself that saved me, or did an Angel pull me out of the seat. All I remembered before the accident is someone pulled me down to the floor before impact. Either way, God had plans to use my life, rather than letting me die in the mountains of Alabama that pitch black night.

A few weeks after the accident, Marlene and I moved to West Virginia with her ex-boyfriend, until I could find somewhere for us to live. He lived in a trailer in a coal mining camp near Beckley, West Virginia.

I wasn't too thrilled, but knew it was a great thing for Eric to be closer to his father since he hadn't seen him in a few years. To me family is the most important thing in the world; I wouldn't keep any son away from his father.

I was very happy for Eric, when we got to his father's house, you could just see the glow on his little face when he got to see his dad again. I was very happy for that!

Marlene's pregnancy went by so fast. Since we knew our baby would be a girl, we wrote names on the wall in our bedroom every time we came up with one. In a sea of names "Paris Tiffany" stood out the most, that's what we named our little Angel.

Since the day she was conceived, I'd lie by her mommy's belly, and talk with her. She'd always answer me back by kicking me.

Near Marlene's due date, my parents wanted to visit to see their grandchild's birth. When they arrived we met them at a hotel, and all went out to a steak house for dinner. Marlene drank her water, her refill, then everyone else's water. After dinner, we said our goodbyes and went home.

By the time Marlene and I went to bed her water broke. Her bags were packed, so I helped her get ready. My dad and mom met us at the house, to take us to the hospital.

Time dragged by as we waited at the hospital. Finally, they decided to do a C-section the next day. I got to go into the room with my wife and watch our daughter's birth. They had a cloth petition draped over my wife, so she couldn't see the surgery; I never took my eyes off the doctors and their work.

As I held my wife's hand, I could see concern in her eyes. I smiled at her and said, *"Everything is okay, honey. It won't be long."*

I don't know how I did it, but my wife's soft brown eyes locked with mine; I knew I needed to keep my composure for her.

It seemed like forever as they prepped her, and drew the line where they would make the incision on her belly. I looked at my wife in the eyes, gave her a big smile, to let her know everything would be fine. Once again, the spirit of joy came over me; I sensed she saw the light in me.

The doctor made the cut, Paris entered the world. Her cry overwhelmed me with joy. I never left my wife's side as they sewed her up. After they moved her into recovery, I kissed her goodbye, and said, *"I'll be back in about half an hour."*

Eric and I went to a flower store; I bought Marlene a dozen roses. Eric bought a teddy bear to give to Paris. When we returned, I saw Marlene was sleeping, so Eric went with my parents back to their room to get some rest.

I sat with my wife, and didn't leave her side until she was released, except for sleeping off and on in the waiting room. I went outside to get some fresh air, I saw an elderly man standing by his car looking confused.

"Are you okay?" I said.

He looked at me with droopy eyes and said, "My wife is dying."

I looked in his car, saw a woman slumped over in the front seat. I ran around the car, opened the door, picked her up in my arms, and then rushed into the emergency room.

That night a nurse came up to me and said, "You saved that woman."

It was such a blessing, to be in the right place, at the right time.

'What I Learned Under the Sun', is God places people together at the right moment in time. His timing is perfect!

Chapter Five

BED & BREAKFAST

When my wife and Paris got out of the Hospital, and started recovering, I called a whitewater rafting company to apply for training to be a whitewater guide. It sounded fun. I liked wild adventure. So, the company hired me. They also hired me to handle their outfitter store sales.

One day as I drove to work, I realized I'd get there too early. So, I stopped at a restaurant for coffee, I was reading the local newspaper, it advertised a twenty-three-room Victorian Home in Fayetteville, West Virginia.

After work that day I showed the house to my wife. We called on it that night and bought it on sight the next day. I don't think it took us more than a few hours, to move all our stuff into the house.

It needed some tender loving care, we thought it would be a great Bed & Breakfast, but it would take a year to remodel the twenty-three-rooms in that Victorian Home. We decided to name it, *"Paris Tiffany's Bed & Breakfast"*—after our daughter.

While working, and training with a Navy Seal to run the river, I only had a few hours in the evenings to spend with Paris and Eric. When my wife and I went to bed, Paris always woke up, and wanted me to pick her up.

I couldn't get out of the bed fast enough to grab Paris out of the crib, so she could lay with me in my arms. I didn't sleep much, however, as I feared rolling over on her. Every night, she slept cradled in my arms like an angel.

Some nights she'd fall back to sleep, and I'd place her back in her crib, so I could be close to my wife. Since Marlene and I got married everything started to look up for us. I always gave the credit to moving away, but looking back, things seemed brighter when we turned from living a life in sin.

It was like after our marriage, God was closing one door after another, and opening all the right ones. We were getting one blessing after another, with all the blessings in our life, our family clung tightly together.

After we got into the house, it was springtime. We spent every day remodeling each room except for our bedroom. We decided we'd do that last, since it was more important to do the guest rooms and common area.

I spent the entire summer guiding the river and working in the outfitter store, which occupied most of my time. I was truly looking forward to fall getting here, so the end of the season would be over. During the winter we could get the twenty-three-rooms in that Victorian Home completely done, so we could open our bed-and-breakfast up in the springtime.

I didn't know much about the rafting industry starting out, but by the end of the summer Marlene and I figured out the market, which strategies other outfitters used, and how we could utilize those strategies for our bed-and-breakfast.

We couldn't open a rafting guide service, because the State of West Virginia, wouldn't allow any other permits, to run rafting trips on the New River. We could, however, open a fishing guide service; we acquired a license to run fishing trips for the next spring season. So we adopted that as our strategy, to opening up a fishing guide service in the spring, use the winter months to book fishing trips and guests into our bed-and-breakfast.

Marlene and I studied the market and the competition's brochures; looking for anything we could utilize that would benefit our success. Then Marlene remembered the many calls we received at our bed-and-breakfast, when we hooked up our phone line; of people wanting to stay with us, and to be booked for their rafting trips.

That was the key. Every rafting company had an 800 number; they all tried to have the word raft in their phone numbers. I called the 800 phone service, by sheer luck the number 1-800-RAFT-WVA was available, and we secured it. Almost immediately, we received calls to book rafting trips.

The best part, is when people called for us to book their rafting trips, they also wanted to stay in our bed-and-breakfast after talking with us on the phone.

We went to every rafting company around Fayetteville, West Virginia, offering them a booking service, for ten percent of the revenues, from customers we would book from our new 800 number. Most of them laughed at us, but three out of the twenty companies signed up with our service.

With three diverse companies, we were able to send the right groups, to the right rafting companies, when they booked trips for customers. Best of all, they were genuinely happy to use our service.

Most of the customers said, they chose staying at our bed-and-breakfast because of our personalities, we handled all the needs for their groups. How convenient, we booked whitewater rafting trips for three companies, fishing trips for our company; and we lodged everyone in our bed-and-breakfast when they came into town.

It seemed like winter flew by, and springtime was almost here. The company I worked for called, 'New Gauley Expeditions' turned all the buying over to me, leaving a ton of inventory from last year. I had to figure out what inventory we had and what I needed to purchase for the new rafting season.

Marlene and I took Paris and Eric to work one night, we went through lines of clothing that didn't sell the previous year. Marlene came up with a brilliant idea to make a hanging raft, (rack, for cloths) out of copper tubing near the cash register. We put all the old merchandise on the hanging raft to move it out.

Marlene redesigned the entire store and merchandising displays. It took us all night. The next morning the owner came in, when he walked in the store, he had this like "wow" look on his face, he couldn't believe we spent the entire night transforming his outfitter store into something so spectacular.

The first weekend his sales went up one-hundred-and-sixty-percent. We blew through merchandise every weekend; I had vendors coming in every Monday morning, the sales for the entire season skyrocketed. I gave all the credit to my wife. The way she displayed the merchandise, her ideas, everything she did made all the difference in the world. I truly think my wife found her calling in life; retail merchandising.

On top of working for a company in the rafting industry, I had my own fishing guide service, travel agency/booking service, and still had to get our bed-and-breakfast done for springtime bookings.

After each day working in the outfitter store, I worked on my fishing guide service, secured rafts, sponsors, guides, and organized media events for springtime.

I also scheduled three TV Celebrities to come in fishing with me to promote my guide service—something never done in this industry.

With the season in full swing the best way to describe our daily life was "hectic" to say the least. Every day was a new adventure on the river; guiding, fishing, and living the life of running a bed-and-breakfast and entertaining guests every night.

Some very colorful customers came into the bed-and-breakfast. Once we had a group of body builders come in. Three guys and one girl decided to stay another night. The next day my wife cleaned their rooms after they left. She came downstairs and said, "You aren't going to believe this. There was only one bed messed up. They all slept in the same bed."

Then some guys came in from New Jersey, and wanted to know if we would like to test some wine. Marlene and I looked at each other. I thought, *'Sure bring in a bottle, we'll drink it with you'*. They brought in a case of wine. We sat up with them until four in the morning. I got an hour sleep, and then had to guide them. That was one long day on the river.

Marlene once booked a man and his son. On their last day at the bed-and-breakfast, the man wanted me to give him a tour of the home. He wanted to see everything. My wife, Eric and Paris were in the living room when he asked me to come into the kitchen with him.

I guess you could say a guy who drove a Mercedes, offered me an indecent proposal. He offered me his car, check for a million dollars, if I would just "walk away" from the bed-and-breakfast and my family.

He looked at me, but not in my eyes, more like through me, and said, "I want what you have, I'll pay you a million dollars for your house, wife, and daughter. All you and your son have to do is take the check, get in my car, drive away, and start a new life."

Wow, I thought. My family isn't for sale, and then kicked the guy out! I couldn't believe this man thought he could buy happiness.

'What I Learned Under the Sun', is Love can't be bought, earned, or inherited. It's a gift from the Lord. If you wait on Him, He will bring

you your soul mate (helpmate) in mind, body, and spirit. You can't buy happiness.

Like I said; we had some very colorful guests come into the bed-and-breakfast to stay with us, some of my favorite times were with a friend of mine; Nick, who brought his entire family. We truly enjoyed their company. Nick was just an awesome guy, had a great family; we loved when they came in to stay with us.

Marlene and I had some very nice people stay with us, who will always be in our hearts. We found no greater joy than during the holidays. We received so many Christmas cards from people who we made friends with, that stayed at our bed-and-breakfast.

I'm sure we left some lasting impressions on a lot of our guests.

We were sent many invitations to stay with people if we ever traveled to their areas. We could actually travel from Florida to Maine, and never book a room with all the invitations from guests that had stayed with us.

Speaking of these wonderful people, one winter we were struggling financially, and didn't have any food. We received a ham gift from UPS. I tried to find out who sent it, but couldn't.

What a blessing we found that to be on Christmas Day. I'm pretty sure a guest sent it, but it could have been a neighbor. Needless to say, we were very blessed. In my heart, I thanked them and blessed them.

Since then, I have paid acts of random kindness forward, every chance I am given an opportunity to help someone in need.

I hope someday that anonymous gift sender will know how much that meant to my family. That their one "Act of Random Kindness" has been passed onto multiple families and individuals by me, from that one good deed.

'What I Learned Under the Sun', is that random acts of kindness, comes from your heart. That a secret under the sun, is showing unconditional love towards one another.

By placing yourself in a positive frame of mind through gratitude, you position yourself to receive blessings on top of blessings, then your heart opens up, and you poor out those blessings onto others, which can only come from your heart!

Chapter Six

WHITEWATER RAFTING

In the beginning God created the "Heavens and Earth," and the New River. Not only is the New River one of the oldest flowing rivers in the world, it also has some of the most majestic scenery to be found anywhere. It's thousand-foot canyon walls and abundant smallmouth fishery is incredible.

Having fished with customers coming from Mexico to Maine, I will take you on some of my most memorable float fishing trips on the New River.

At an early age, I learned something valuable, but never realized it until I became a professional guide. The old saying; "We have eyes but cannot see, we have ears but cannot hear." Well I'm here to tell you it plays a major part in the success of any fishing trip.

If we look at what nature tells us our success rate improves dramatically. I knew before I got to the rolling waters of the river, what kind of day a customer would have depending on whether we saw any wildlife on the way to the put-in site.

If we saw wildlife moving in the dark while heading to the river we could be assured that when the sun rose over the canyon walls we'd hear birds chirping, and see ducks flying overhead. Then I knew it'd be only a matter of time before my clients were hooking into some citation (trophy) smallmouth.

On the other hand, if I saw no sign of wildlife I knew we would have a very long day on the river. Mother Nature is always right. She is splendid and does work in mysterious ways.

Springtime fluttered into our lives, the first customers scheduled to come in fishing with me, was the TV Celebrity Billy Westmoreland, otherwise known as; "The Smallmouth King." You would never meet a more humble man in your life.

Once when we were on the river, the mud thickened the water. I looked in my tackle box, found green florescent crank bait, thinking that would do the job in the high water conditions. The first pool we approached, I landed a citation smallmouth on national TV. That fish looked like a monster. When I unhooked the fish and released it, Billy said, "Hey Kyle, let me have one of those crank baits."

We both got double headers (both of us getting fish on at the same time), it didn't take long for Billy to cast beside a dead fall that laid silently in a pool on the river's edge. Almost, as soon as his lure hit the water, he hooked into his first citation fish. By the end of the day we caught well over one hundred smallmouth bass.

You know, you have those days when you do everything right, and nothing can go wrong. Sort of like, how I would describe the first four years since Marlene and I were married. What it took to get here and how we did it. We enjoyed life so much our smiles probably added so many creases to our faces, we were so happy.

When Billy and I returned to the bed-and-breakfast that night, my wife waited for us with her famous lasagna dinner, complete with homemade rolls. Due to the heavy rain all day, she worried, that the river would rise and shut the fish down, but she could tell by the expression on my face that Billy and I had an awesome day. I couldn't stop smiling.

Marlene looked at me, said, "You didn't out-fish Billy, did you?"
"Not too bad," I said. "It was like three-to-one and I got the biggest one."

After dinner I had a press conference scheduled for Billy. At the end of the conference, he had pictures taken with all of us. Our son Eric loved it, and Paris, well; the only celebrity in her life was her dad.

Billy and his crew left later that night, at about one in the morning, I received a fax from Billy that he made it home safely. He thanked us for a great trip, our hospitality, and my wife's wonderful home cooked food.

It wasn't only her cooking. She had a sweet personality that everyone loved. Her ability to present things never ceased to amaze me. She could present something as simple as butter with such talent that it became attractive to people. Everything she created looked perfect, almost as if God gave her a gift, coming straight from her heart.

What a wild ride the summer had been on the New River. Marlene and I prepared for a trip to Las Vegas, to attend ICAST; the sportfishing industry's largest trade event. A major catalyst for sales and a terrific networking opportunity for the sportfishing community. We wanted to sell our float fishing trips, so she designed a magnificent brochure for us that screamed *FUN*.

Most people had a product in their booths, but we sold excitement, adventure, and memories that would last a lifetime. She came up with the idea to use silk draped over cardboard, on a small stand with a large gift certificate, surrounded with green gemstones, and our brochure displayed on the stand.

I watched in awe at her beautiful ability to conceptualize something so fast, but still so professional and appealing. I finally confirmed in my mind that her spiritual gift had to be retail and hospitality.

During the flight my wife slept in my arms. I watched her, thinking over the last few years since we were married, and how truly blessed our family had been.

I don't know if it happened the day we got married, when God made His presence known or the day He saved me in Alabama. Either way, life couldn't have been better.

Marlene held my sweaty palm as we both leaned forward while the 747 landed on the runway. Finally, we were in Las Vegas for the July ICAST Show. At the carousel for our bags, I leaned over, kissed Marlene, and said, *"We forgot to get our wings on this flight."*

She smiled and said, "Wait until we get to the room." I'm like right; husbands, don't like to wait . . .

We scheduled a dinner meeting with Babe Winkelman and his wife for that evening. After we got settled in and freshened up, we took a cab to their hotel to meet them. Standing in the lobby there were various people around a huge slot machine. For some reason I had a feeling it would pay off, so I gave Marlene twenty dollars to give it a try.

One dollar remained in her credit. She put her hand on the lever to pull and I said, "Wait. Put in two more dollars and bet max." I handed her the crumpled bills. She put them in, pulled the handle, buzzers went off, people hooted and hollered, as three red sevens lined up on the slot machine. Marlene won the jackpot!

Mrs. Winkelman walked up and said, "We're ready".

"Just a minute," I said. "Marlene has to collect her winnings."

The minute turned into a half hour, while Babe waited outside for us. When we got into the car we told Babe the story, he laughed and said, "I've waited for a lot of things in my day, but never for a woman to collect a jackpot."

I still couldn't believe Marlene won. I was so happy for her. At dinner we discovered that the four of us had so much in common, from what we drank, to what we ate. All of our personalities clicked in perfect harmony.

Babe agreed to bring his crew to our bed-and-breakfast next March, which seemed far off, in terms of time. After dinner we went with them to the casino so Babe and I could try out our luck. I'm sure he won, but I didn't win anything.

At the end of the night Marlene and I hugged them goodbye, went to a quiet lounge where we sat next to each other, talking about our marriage, and how everything seemed to be going really good for us the last few years.

What a night we experienced. In the morning I woke up with Marlene in my arms. I gently swept her blond hair behind her ear, as she slept so peacefully, giving her a gentle kiss good morning.

Instantly my thoughts, raced back to Alabama, where we conceived Paris, then looked at Marlene's beautiful face and kissed her forehead.

"Honey," I said. "It's time to wake up. We have to get ready for the show."

She didn't seem to want to move, so I rolled her over, gave her a morning massage that led us to being late for the first day of the show.

We booked a lot of trips at the show, scheduled two National TV shows to come in and film. Not a bad week. Publicity definitely proved to be worth its weight in gold. So, I guess we left Vegas as big winners.

Summer brought on the heat; and we were in full swing running guided fishing trips. Our bed-and-breakfast had no vacancies every day of the summer. We were booked solid. Each day, while guiding on the New River, I never knew what kind of adventure awaited me.

One time I had a couple come in, and while we were on the river, the Corps of Engineers decided to open the floodgates. As I looked around, I saw a dramatic change in the currents, and the river filling with debris.

"I have some good news and some bad news," I told my guests. Neither of them had any idea what I meant. The beautiful sunny sky reflected off the river. Everything seemed peaceful and perfect going down the river to the customers.

One of them said, "What's the bad news"?

"Look around. The river is coming up fast, I think you're about to take the whitewater ride of your life with me."

"What's the good news?"

"You can have a refund and still have your steak dinner tonight, if we make it out alive." I smiled. "Make sure you get on your PFD's, hold on, and get ready for the wildest whitewater rafting trip you'll ever have in your life."

They looked at each other, then looked me in the eyes, realizing, I wasn't joking. It took me a few seconds, to tie everything down. About that time a huge tree floated by our raft.

"Oh, crap," I heard one of the guys say.

During a dam release, class III's become class V's, which are only maneuverable by an expert, with the chance of loss of life or limbs. Immediately, I got us into the main wave train, of the river, and entire trees passed by us in the raging river.

It was a very lonely day on the river, since we were the only ones there. The first class V I came to it was difficult to see the rapids as the water was raging so fast. I knew if I didn't hit it just right we were in deep trouble.

After I made it through those rapids, the entire river became a class V. I felt like I was tossed into a giant blender, not knowing which way to go, the waves were so big. With all my might, I tried to keep us in the wave train in the middle of a raging river.

Almost too hard to describe, the best way is, I would say grab yourself a tire inner tube, be dropped off by a helicopter in the middle of Lake Michigan during one of the worst storms, then try to paddle to shore.

What should have been a ten-hour float trip, took us less than an hour. When we got to the takeout my body ached from guiding that morning. I'd never seen two guys, whiter than ghosts and happier, than those two customers when they saw our van at the takeout.

When I loaded up the raft on the van I looked back at the river, another tree was floating by and gone in a matter of seconds around the bend. I thought to myself, 'how lucky we were.'

When we got back to the bed-and-breakfast, I called the river levels, it had crested over twenty-three feet above normal pool from when we started.

I thought, 'well, the Lord definitely stood by me.' If the raft would, have flipped in those conditions, we would have died on the river that morning.

Try swimming a class V rapid. It's hard enough trying to get safely back to the raft if it flips, much less rescue a customer in the water. At those levels it's nearly impossible, and we were the only people on the river that day.

A few weeks later, the customers came back and booked another trip with me. The three of us had a special bond together, that you could feel in the air. It was like there was a mist coming off the canyon walls. You could just feel a higher power in our presence that morning, we all felt a truly sense of peace on the river.

We all gave thanks to the Lord and felt like He watched over us, smiling as we viewed the most magnificent sun rise over the canyon walls that morning. It looked like the most beautiful painting of colorful clouds with the sun's rays beaming through.

It was as if you just knew and felt that it was going to be a great day on the river fishing. No matter who came in to fish or stayed with us, we always tried to do something above and beyond what they expected.

When customers left our bed-and-breakfast, we wanted them to feel as if they were leaving home, knowing that they had made friends for life.

Another time, a friend of ours, Steve, came in from the Bassmaster's Circuit with his wife Lorraine. Marlene and I took them fishing. Later in the day he boasted about all the fish he caught.

Marlene said, "Kyle, get up there and show him how to catch fish." Steve's wife agreed.

Marlene took over the helm at the oars and I got my special fishing rod out.

"Get fishing," Steve said.

"I will," I said. *"I'm just waiting for the right moment."*

I looked downstream and saw a beautiful shoot come up, with a nice-looking eddy on the right of the river. "Honey," I said. "Are you okay? Can you drop us in that shoot?"

She smiled. "No problem."

As Marlene dropped us into the shoot, I cast towards the eddy, as soon as the lure hit the water a five-pound smallmouth nailed it. Our wives went crazy when I landed it, we all laughed at Steve because I made one cast and caught the biggest fish of the day. The best part was the women kept reminding him who caught the biggest fish for the rest of the day.

Some of my favorite trips were when I had one customer come in and could bring Eric with me. Every time we got back, he ran up to his mother and said, *"I out-fished Dad again today."*

Eric always out-fished me. I loved the look on the boy's face every time he caught a fish, especially when he got to go with me on the river all day.

When we got off the river today, Eric and I walked into the house my wife looked stunning. I thought we had another celebrity coming in and

I had forgot about it. Her hair was done up perfect and she had on a new dress that took my breath away.

Marlene walked up to me and touched her lips to mine. I saw a nice dinner set on the table as she smiled and said, "I'm pregnant!"

I held back tears of joy, hugged her, then said; *"I love you so much."*

In her tone, I sensed she might have been nervous about my reaction. In bed that night I thanked God for the great news.

Just like we did for Paris, we wrote names on the wall, everyone in the family got involved this time. I think we had the best wall for a headboard in the world. Out of the hundreds of choices, we chose the name, Skyler Marquise. Overwhelmed with joy, I couldn't wait to call our parents.

The next day my friends from Howmet, Dave and Linda, called. They wanted to come down and visit. We couldn't wait to see them. There's no better way to catch up for lost time than float down a river all day.

The next few weeks we didn't have too many trips to do or customers coming in to stay. That gave us more time to get ready for Dave and Linda's visit.

It was pretty exciting when they got there since I hadn't seen them in so long. Dave and I spent many times together riding Harley's, I'm sure I could write a book about our entire road trips we went on together.

Like always we stayed up way too late, when they got in, but Eric and I had already gotten the raft and equipment ready before they arrived.

We spent the next day floating and messing around on the New River, making a lot of stops, while Linda took pictures everywhere. I told them about running whitewater, if they were adventurous they could ride the bull, when we run a class V rapid.

"What's the Bull?" Linda said.

"That's when you sit on the front of the raft, with your legs hanging over, hang on to a rope tied to the d-ring." Then see, if you can hang on!

Linda said, "Sounds like fun. I'm in."

I set Linda up before we were about to drop into class V rapids. When I hit the first wave, the raft dropped down, she disappeared over the front of the raft. I jumped up, dove for the front of the raft, reached under it and grabbed her life jacket. I flipped her back into the boat and got back to guiding us through the rest of the rapids.

Dave never even knew she went out of the raft, it happened so fast. Her eyes were comparable to the size of silver dollars, as she sat down and hugged her arms around her waist. I'll always remember the look of shock on Linda's face, when I flipped her back into the raft. Definitely a memorable trip, for all of us!

Soon after they left, another company called, wanting me to guide a trip for them. I agreed, when I got to the river, I had a raft full of college girls, looking for adventure. They couldn't understand what river left or river right was. I imagined, it would be a long day.

At the first class V, I screamed for them to paddle river left. They went the opposite way, we hit the wave train sideways. It flipped our raft. I tried, without success to save seven girls floating down the river but thankfully other rafts came over to help out.

After we got to shore, I stood there with seven dripping wet, ticked off girls, who refused to get back into my raft. We had seven miles of river to go. "It's the only way out," you take the river, or walk the railroad tracks at the bottom of the canyon."

They wouldn't get back in with me, so I walked them out. That was the longest seven miles, I've ever walked. My wife came to the outfitter to pick me up, when the trip got back and realized I wasn't there. One guide told her I had problems on the river—flipped or something.

She later told me she said, "Well, where is he?"

The kid said, "I don't know. He didn't make it out."

Soon about to give birth, she lived a nightmare all over again. She knew death, haunted the river every year. And not knowing where her husband was didn't ease her mind. She looked for every guide on the trip, finally found out that I flipped the boat and had to walk the group out.

The girls and I finally made it out. I don't think I've ever seen my wife so happy to see me, yet very, very mad at the same time.

She made me promise to stop guiding wild rides. It's the only section of the river I wouldn't let her or my boy go down, because I couldn't save them, if I flipped out of the boat. The river is particularly wild during high water in the springtime.

Another day on the river, I had a woman ask me, where was the safest place to sit in the raft. "Next to the guide," I said.

Big mistake, every time we hit rapids, I flew out of the raft, and had like seven near-death experiences in one day. I thought it was one of those days where nothing went right, but when I reviewed the video after the trip, it revealed a woman getting down on her knees before I hit the rapids. The force threw her into me, causing me to fly out of the raft all day.

Life is short. It's amazing how fast time flies. March was here, faster than we could blink and our daughter Skyler, came into the world. I never prayed so hard in my life, than when she was born. I shed more tears of joy, than all the water I've swallowed guiding all those years.

When Marlene got home everyone hovered over her.

Then I said, "Oh, by the way, honey,"

"Babe and his camera crew will be here next week."

Babe Winkelman hosts two of the most-watched outdoor television shows in history: "Good Fishing" and "Outdoor Secrets."

Marlene made me work my butt off, to prepare for them coming in. I didn't want her doing anything anyway. She needed to rest, take care of Skyler, our newest angel in the family.

We bought new furniture and carpet for Babe's room; it never came before I had to leave for the airport to pick up Babe. When I left, it finally arrived. Marlene, the angel she was, laid the carpet and had his room ready when we got home. She even had that happy smile on her face when we came in the door from the airport.

Chapter Seven

NATIONAL TV APPEARANCES

My guides and I spent most of the evening getting equipment ready for a two day trip in the morning with Babe and his crew. We had five rafts going out. The first day of fishing we didn't fare well, but oh what a night of camping we experienced.

It took us a while to set up everything. The fire blazed with readiness for our steaks. Marlene sent some homemade brownies for the crew. Not just any brownie—they were exceptional. After everyone had one, I hid the rest in my tent.

Later, everyone asked where the rest of the brownies went.

"I don't have a clue," I said.

An old tree that overlooked the river surrounded our tents. The producer wanted to knock it down for firewood since it was dead. As it was swaying back and forth a rattlesnake slithered beside my tent. We figured there were probably more in the tree, so we left it alone.

The sun set over the canyon walls. Babe disappeared, then snuck behind me, and tapped me on the ankle with a stick. I flung backwards about ten feet, as everyone laughed. I thought for sure a snake bit me. Everyone literally laughed so hard they cried, which is probably why Babe tried it a few more times during the night.

We managed to wake in the morning without any incidents with snakes. Our Guides prepared a huge breakfast for us, supplied by our caterer.

After the guides got everything packed back into the rafts we got on the river again. I don't even think Babe's raft had pulled away from the shore yet and he already had a citation fish on.

The entire day was on and off again rain. I tried my hardest to catch a monster smallmouth, but Babe was the only one that got the big ones, that day.

It was an awesome day on the river and everyone caught fish. We had a great time filming on the New River. When we returned to the bed-and-breakfast, Marlene smiled and unpacked my duffel bag.

"Why is the brownie pan in here?" she asked.

I laughed. *"They were great, dear."*

Everyone got unpacked from the river, showered, and back into dry cloths. Marlene had a huge dinner prepared for everyone. It was very special, sitting around the candlelit table, talking about the trip, about how we met in Las Vegas, and how much fun that it was.

The next morning Babe and his crew prepared to leave. Our two oldest kids Eric and Paris wanted pictures with Babe, so they got up early and patiently waited on the sofa for him to come downstairs.

Babe's wife; Kris, came down first, as she came into the kitchen, she said, "Your kids are so polite. I came through the living room and they both said, "Good morning, ma'am."

We couldn't ask for better kids living in a bed-and-breakfast.

The kids got their pictures, as they always did with celebrities. We hugged everyone goodbye, then Marlene gave each of them, a brown paper bag full of homemade chocolate chip cookies she baked the night before, for their trip home.

The camera crew left with huge smiles on their faces. We were truly sad to see them leave. You couldn't meet a nicer couple in the world than Babe and Kris, and their entire camera crew was a joy to have around.

Soon after Babe and Kris left, another celebrity, Roland Martin, came in and went fishing with me. He was a very good friend of ours, whom I professionally fished with on the Bassmaster's Tournament Trail and FLW Tour.

When Roland got in, we were all happy to see him again. Marlene made him a lasagna dinner that night and we stayed up late catching up on old times.

The next morning we headed to the river's put-in site. I frantically looked for wildlife. Finally, two deer ran in front of us. "Yes," I yelled.

Roland's producer said, "Kyle, if we don't get any fish today, we're not going to get a show." With the wildlife out, I knew, it would be an awesome day on the river.

It didn't take us long to start hooking into fish, I couldn't even count all the double headers we had throughout the day. It was another one of those colder days on the river with, off and on again, rain.

The river was in perfect condition to catch fish, when we got on the river, we caught loads of fish. Roland even got a few Muskie's, a fish of a thousand casts; I think it took Roland two casts. The show turned out so well that he put me on the intro-video, for his famed TV Show for an entire year.

We had a great time, but they were glad to get off the river when it started to get bitterly cold as the sun disappeared behind the canyon walls.

My wife had dinner ready when we returned.

Roland said to her, "Your husband is an animal." He stood on the shore in shorts while the cold rain poured down and the guides built a fire under a rock cliff to keep us out of the weather.

We held another press conference and Marlene prepared a huge spread for the media. As I got ready in the bedroom, she walked in and said, "You're not going to believe what happened today."

"What?" I said.

"While I was cooking, the furnace went out, I had to take it apart and fix it."

I hugged her and thanked her. It sounded like she had a long, rough day, and should have put a sign on the front door that read: *"Gone shopping. Fend for yourselves!"*

After the press conference Roland took pictures with our kids. They got the biggest kick out of taking those pictures. Their baby books are loaded with portraits of celebrities they've been with at our bed-and-breakfast.

Roland and his crew left the next day, with their bag of homemade cookies, to fish the Top 100 on the Connecticut River. I talked with him a few weeks later, he told me he won the competition. I must have done well teaching him how to fish smallmouth in the river.

Unknown to us, Marlene and I would be there in a few years, and I would make CNN Headline News in Hartford, Connecticut.

Fall swept the summer away with its crisp weather and the rafting season was winding down. The kids bugged me to take them rafting, so Marlene and I took them on a picnic to the lake. I paddled them across the lake to a waterfall, then back which was quite relaxing for me rather than running the wild rapids every day.

In West Virginia deer season was about to begin. One of our guides wanted to go deer hunting in the mountains.

"Why not," I said. "Sounds like another adventure."

The next week Marlene took us to an old mining camp the morning before opening day. She dropped us off and we hiked in from there. I told her to come back with the kids before dark, I'd walk them in, and we'd have a bon fire.

I hiked back out to the mine, an hour before dark, soon after Marlene pulled in with the kids. All the kids were excited. Marlene had a bag for me to carry with all kinds of goodies for the night.

The hike to the camp took awhile. At times we bent down and crawled through the thick underbrush. I carried Skyler in one hand and the bag in the other. Marlene, Eric, and Paris followed down the trail.

Darkness edged the horizon with only a hint of the sun's rays peeking through. We finally saw the campsite. Jody, our guide, had a fire blazing. He was a true woodsman, even looked like a Wildman. As we walked into camp, he sat and picked his teeth with a buck knife.

Marlene brought all the kids marshmallows, my darling Paris would eat one, then burn the next one, and fling it into the woods.

They stayed a few hours until it became very dark. I think the kids were scared of all the noises in the mountains, and wanted to leave. We had to walk about a mile out of the mountains, in total darkness with one flashlight, which Marlene held. She walked behind me. I carried Skyler, Paris was on my back, and she practically choked me to death as she clung to my neck. We heard so many cracks in the woods, like sticks breaking and wild animal sounds. When Eric saw the van he ran for it.

I got everyone in the van. Marlene and the kids tried to talk me into coming home, but I couldn't leave Jody out in the middle of the woods alone. Hard telling what kind of trouble he'd get into.

"No worries honey," I said. "I'll see you tomorrow night."

I could see in Paris' eyes that she didn't want me to stay. I assured her not to worry about daddy, that I'd see her tomorrow when they came back to roast marshmallows again.

After they left, I walked down the trail. About a half mile into the forest my flashlight went out. I smacked it in my hand to get it to work again. When the light hit my hand, I heard a big snort in the woods beside me. I turned but couldn't see anything, except utter darkness, I could feel in my gut that something was there.

I felt around and broke off a large stick, which I used to stay on the trail. Whatever I heard in the woods followed me. When I'd walk, it would walk; when I stopped it would stop.

It took some time to get down the trail and back to camp. A huge smile warmed my face when I finally saw the fire off in the distance. I walked faster; let me tell you, I made double time back to that fire. Thankfully, I was finally at the campsite.

Jody and I stayed up for a few more hours, and then he went to bed. I checked the other tent to make sure we didn't leave any food out. I went in the tent and saw Jody in his sleeping bag while cooking stew on a small stove. What is this moron doing? "Don't be cooking food in my tent."

I climbed in my sleeping bag to warm up. It was so cold I could see my breath. About four hours later Jody woke me up, saying, "Kyle, wake up. Kyle, wake up. There's a deer outside!"

"Well, shoot it," I said, then rolled back over.

He shook me frantically. "It's right outside the door."

"So, shoot him already."

He held his shotgun in his hand, bent over to unzip the door. I climbed out of my sleeping bag and heard Jody yell, *"Bear!"*

Reacting on impulse, I accidentally kicked Jody in the butt; he tumbled out the tent door, rolled down a little incline, and ran into the bear. His gun went off. I jumped out of the tent. From the light of the fire, I saw the bear run one way and Jody run the other way screaming his lungs out.

I stood there in the dark of the night in my underwear and laughed my butt off. Jody whined like a big baby because I pushed him into the bear. I got dressed and Jody put all the wood we had on the fire, still crying like a baby.

Neither of us slept the rest of the night.

Jody asked again, "Why the heck, did you kick me?"

"Because I didn't want the bear in the tent with me and I knew I could out run you." I laughed again.

We heard what seemed like a million crunches in the woods. The both of us stayed close to the fire as it lit up the woods for the rest of the night.

I thought about the marshmallows Paris tossed into the woods. The bear probably was watching us as I walked my family out in the dark. I imagined walking them out and having a three-hundred-pound bear step out in front of Marlene. Yeah. Wow!!!

The next morning I took a picture of a 12-pack that the bear clawed. His paw marks were as wide as the 12-pack in the snow. I must say, the bear was lucky he didn't paw at me in the middle of the night. He would of had a heart attack from Jody's piercing screams.

After a sleepless night, daylight finally broke through and we hunted. I found a ridge to sit on, five minutes later a deer walked through the bottom of the ridge, turned, and came straight at me, a nice four-point deer.

It looked right at me, so I couldn't pull my gun up to shoot it. Then, it walked within ten feet of me, got on its knees, rested on the ground, and buried its head between its legs. All I could see were horns sticking out of its body.

I sat there for what seemed like hours, watching the deer sleep. Sometimes it lifted its head and looked around, but never turned to see me sitting there. The wind blew in my face so the deer couldn't smell me.

I could hardly hold my breath. A million thoughts ran through my head. *Do I shoot it? Do I wait for it to run and give it a chance?* So, I decided to shoot it. We needed the food for winter.

That night when my wife and kids got there I took their offer, loaded up the deer and went home with them. I had enough adventure for one day from that bear last night! They didn't want anything to do with walking through the woods after they heard about the bear story.

Back at home Eric and I hung the deer up in a tree, and then unloaded the van. I was exhausted from no sleep the night before, so off to bed I went.

With another rafting season behind us, after Christmas we decided to sell the bed-and-breakfast and move back to Michigan. I had some sponsors lined up to fish professionally.

Then it hit me, I skipped out on the court date, many years ago, so I called my lawyer friend Harold and told him that I was coming back, he said, "When you get here come see me and we'll see what we can do to fix the problem for failure to appear."

It didn't take us long at all to sell out to the competition and move back to Michigan. I met my lawyer and ended up getting three days for the charge I had skipped out on.

My lawyer then told me if you don't get in any more trouble for another ten years, your record will be clean.

I landed some sponsors, and then started working on getting everything ready to go on tour. My wife and I had to go to Kentucky, to sign up for the FLW Tour. One of my first tournaments was in Missouri; we took the kids with us to stay in a condo.

They had a blast; they got to see all the celebrities that fished with dad and got more pictures taken. My wife always cooked them dinner on the road, they would all pay her for her hospitality. They would tell me they were just chipping in for the food I bought.

The condo overlooked the lake; my family said an eagle was outside the window hovering, while I was fishing. As it turned out, it was one of the best days I had fishing in that tournament.

I had a tournament in New York where my wife and I stayed with a sponsor. The fishing sucked, but she had a blast going with the wives everyday sightseeing and touring castles. Marlene always has wanted to live in a castle. All I had to do was win a tournament for my princess so I could afford it.

A few years back at the bed-and-breakfast, I said we'd be in Connecticut fishing someday! Well we made it! During the four days of pre-practice, I'm on fish big time. So much so, that I'm pretty positive I'd win this tournament and buy my Cinderella her castle.

Tournament day arrives. With very little sleep we headed to the put-in site, as we pulled in, I was in awe. During the night it rained upstream. A hundred miles upstream a dam broke and flooded everything.

Not to be discouraged though and because of my previous experiences fishing high water, I blasted off and headed straight to my honey hole. Only to find the island I was limiting out on was flooded with waters raging over it. I still tried to fish the back side, but the fish were gone or had a serious case of lock jaw.

So as a backup plan, I told my amateur partner, "I'm headed to find a creek with clear water, that I passed about five miles downstream." Never having been up the creek, I decided to gun it, and go as far as I could in my Ranger Boat, until I found clear water.

When I hit the creek, I was flying so fast, that I was actually throwing water on the banks as I turned into the corners. I glanced at my partner and smiled, he gave me one of those stares like, "what the heck is this guy doing?"

I made it about three miles up before a log jam prevented me from finding clear water, so I decided to fish out anyways. I'm like, dude aren't you going to fish? He just sat there in his seat, holding on! I'm thinking to myself, "What is the problem, we're here to win this tournament."

When we came back, my wife had CNN headline news interview me about the high water conditions for the tournament, which was pretty cool. My wife and I went out to dinner, and watched it on TV that night in Hartford.

I didn't catch a fish, but we had a great time in Hartford, Connecticut, and I'm still determined more than ever to get my Cinderella her castle. The nice thing about fishing on tour is, it's a family sport, and my kids loved staying in condo's or cabins next to the lakes. Everywhere we went it was like a new adventure for the kids.

Some of the tournaments I fished were; Lake Toho, Wheeler Lake, Kentucky Lake, Forrest Wood Open, Lake St. Clair, Lake of the Ozarks, Buggs Island, California Delta Waterway, Richard B. Russell Lake, Lake Sinclair, St. Lawrence River and Walmart Open.

The last tournament I fished was the Walmart Open; on the Walmart FLW Tour held in Rogers, Arkansas on Beaver Lake. With the water conditions it was tough fishing. I was more fortunate than most of the anglers, and placed in the money earning a $2,000 check.

Chapter Eight

TRAVELS TO EVERY CITY IN AMERICA

Driving home it was exciting, but not enough earnings to buy my princess her castle, so I had to go back to work selling merchandise to Chain Stores. Drinking coffee one morning, I read an advertisement for a National Sales Manager at a local outdoor company that sold paddle boats.

Selling to National Chain stores is my specialty. I enjoyed this very much and my wife and I got to travel, see the country doing manager meetings and tradeshows.

I just finished the season fishing professional on the Walmart FLW Tour and Bass Masters Tournament Trail. So naturally my first call was to Walmart. I flew to Bentonville, Arkansas, Walmarts Home Office, and met with the Boat Buyer.

He called me a few weeks later, notified me to start selling store-direct to thousands of Walmarts. Walmart, was one of my top accounts, I had enjoyed merchandising to them as a supplier over the last ten years.

I divided all the stores up by territories, having every sales person in the department to start calling on Walmarts. Everyone was selling boats like crazy, except for one girl that called every Walmart, in five States, and didn't make one sale. I went to the owner of the company and told him she's got to go. She's not a sales person. His remark was; "Heaven forbid; she's the best I have." I thought to myself; "Wow, she's called five States,' and hasn't had one sale, she's the best you've got."

Every other sales girl was selling boats by the truck loads in their designated States, which pretty much should tell an owner of a company something; you would think.

I told him I'm bringing someone in to call on all the stores in those states that his "best girl" couldn't make a sale in. The only person, I know who has that kind of talent is my wife. So I brought her to work with me. Marlene worked her magic, in the first month of calling those Walmart stores that the girl had no sales in, my wife sold over a half a million dollars in boats.

I was never so proud of my wife in my life, which meant she got hired and we got to do shows together.

I had to go to Chicago, right after she got hired to a sports show. I stayed at the Palmer House and after I got checked in I went out to eat. When I came back into the lobby, I ran into of all people, my ex-girlfriend's (Brenda) parents, Dan and Loretta.

I was very happy to see them, they told me there were no rooms available in town because of the shows, I told them they could have my bed, and I'd have a cot brought up to the room.

How wild is that, being in Chicago and running into your ex-girlfriend's parents, of all people, I thought it was very cool, that I could help them.

Talk about a small world, I loved it. They brought me up-to-date on all the details on how Brenda and Rita were doing; that was very special to my heart.

I called my wife to share my day, told her of the situation at the hotel, running into Brenda's parents and helping them out, her jealously surfaced again in a bursting outrage on the phone.

I was very glad to see them the next morning, they gave me a ride to the show and dropped me off. What a small world it is.

When I got home, I got grief for some time over that, but could never figure out why my wife was mad at me for helping someone out. I almost wish, I wouldn't have said anything, but I've always been honest with my wife. That's the most important element in any relationship.

Our new jobs took us to a lot of exciting tradeshows and cities packed with fun and excitement, over the course of the next year.

Back in Chicago I had to do some business research so we went to the Chicago Public Library to do this. My wife disappeared, came back, and said; "You won't believe this, look what I found."

She found a fishing book about the 1991 World Ice Fishing Championships with a picture of the Russian Team. I was right in the middle of the photograph. I had no clue that photo ever made it in a book. I was impressed she found it.

Another time while everyone was doing their own thing, we spent our time socializing and met the owners of one of the largest sporting goods chain stores in Trader Vic's at the Palmer House. That's what my wife and I did best.

Our personalities attracted all the right people. We were always looking out for each other, we attracted all the right attention at all our business functions. When we worked together as one, the Lord always blessed us in everything we did.

Over the years we went to a lot of tradeshows. I traveled often to meet with major buyers. Two of the largest were Sear's and Costco, whom I convinced to sell Paddle Boats and Canoes. Only to have the owner of the company decide not to ship because of logistics issues.

It's too hard to land national accounts, and then have the owner of the company decide not to sell the product? It kills the reputation of the company, and your reputation, as a top salesperson in the industry. After all the work you do and they have the orders cancelled.

I gave the owner a two-week notice. I landed a job with one phone call to a friend in the Paintball Industry. He wanted to hire me for years after meeting me at a Tradeshow in Atlanta, Georgia.

His booth was across from mine and after the show he invited me to dinner. He told me that I had what he wanted! That all the buyers in the industry were my friends and that's what he wanted for his company, those kinds of relationships.

He knew the value of relationships; they are worth Gold, if you have products to sell in the retail industry. You can have the best product in the world, but if it's not on the store shelves selling, "you've got a problem." That is my specialty, selling to chain stores, that was the attraction for him wanting to hire me. He had wisdom, knowing, I knew all the right people, and I had personal relationships with the buyers.

This was a more fast-paced, aggressive, and highly competitive industry. If you don't land the accounts, you have to wait another year to get your foot in the door. I was constantly on the road, for days on-end, landing new accounts, because every national account was doing their reviews for next year's categories.

Lately, when I started calling home my wife seemed to always be out when I called. Marlene had a new girlfriend in her life coming over and always wanting to talk in private. Then she'd have to take off somewhere. Soon, rumors in our town were going around, she was having an affair.

Ironically, instead of a girlfriend, it was a guy that had befriended her; he always seemed to appear whenever we went somewhere. My wife would disappear or always have to run somewhere for a minute, saying, she'd be right back.

When I came home my kids would always run up to me yelling; "Daddy's Home."

Pretty soon that stopped and when I walked into the house, my wife would not be herself. No more welcome wagon what-so-ever. It was like I didn't exist, I felt as if there was something terribly wrong, but just couldn't put my finger on it. "What was happening?"

My three grueling months of being a road-warrior was over, I landed all the accounts I had targeted and now I could sit back the rest of the summer and just manage the business when issues came up such as production, logistics, or returns.

To me, that was the best part of the job. It gave me lots of time to be with my children, when they were out of school. That's the most gratifying thing in the world to me, being home with my daughters.

One weekend my wife wanted to go to the local rodeo, her friend who thought he was a cowboy, needed a ride. Marlene asked me if we could give him a ride. Well, the day came, he needed a ride, so I agreed to pick him up and he went with our family to the rodeo.

We were sitting in the stands, the cowboy asked my wife if she wanted to go for a walk, she said; "Honey, I'll be right back we have to run to the car for a minute." Then he came back and took my two girls for ice-cream!

After the show, we took him home, in his driveway my wife jumps out, and said; "She had to run in the house for a minute." My kids and I sat in the car for twenty minutes in silence, wondering, and waiting for her to come out.

They say love is blind, to trust your gut feelings. I never would have suspected him, at that time I trusted my wife; she always made it look like it was his roommate that was the snake in the wood pile.

When she followed the guy in the house, I should have put the Jimmy in drive, and drove away with our girl's.

A month later was Marlene's fortieth birthday, knowing how some women tend to have issues with milestone birthdays; I was going to plan a small family gathering.

This cowboy friend of hers, ended up planning a huge party for her. Was my input not needed for such a party? She was still my wife, after all.

I refused to go, and tried to talk her into celebrating it with her family, she said; "screw you, it's my party". This was the start of big problems in our marriage. The trust was destroyed; she never did admit to any wrong doings, she always denied it.

Months earlier, after I had finished my grueling on-the-road marketing schedule, I had planned an Alaskan fishing excursion with my friend Rick.

My wife no longer seemed interested in spending time as a family. I got a call on my cell phone during that trip from some woman who said, Marlene was dating the cowboy. She was all furious with my wife, and told me she just got into an argument with her at our house, of all places. My wife left with her boyfriend, the cowboy. I had no idea how this woman knew my cell phone number, so I called home. No answer. It was one of those nights my wife claimed she didn't hear the phone ring!

Returning home wasn't happy either. I don't know of any person who would be, after the phone call I received. Marlene denied anything ever went on, and she had no idea what the woman was talking about, and said she was just lying to me. I called the woman back, asked her to meet me downtown, and my wife just laughed.

When I left, so did my wife, and never came home all weekend. Sometime after that incident she returned home and took our vehicle. After hours of contemplating our situation, Monday morning came, I walked to our bank, my gut feeling told me that something just wasn't right, and it wasn't. I was not surprised when I reached the bank, Marlene was there parked in the driveway with my Jimmy.

I went to get in it and she had a club locked onto the steering wheel, so that I could not take it. I asked her what she was doing at the bank? and she replied, "I'm taking out all our money."

Marlene made a big scene in the bank demanding the money. The manager wouldn't give either one of us any money at that time and we were asked to leave. We were asked to come back the next afternoon to close the account. The bank was no longer willing to house our account. The manager decided on his own to split the account giving each of us half.

I was now seeing a side of Marlene that I had no clue existed. Money seemed to be her everything. I wasn't that upset, it's only money, that doesn't buy happiness, but I guess for some people it does.

I was mad as heck, she had my Jimmy, the worse part, was the front end of the Jimmy had damage. Marlene stated she had no clue how it happened, I wouldn't find out until years later during our divorce discovery process, that she had gotten into an accident and been arrested for drunk driving.

That's how deceptive my wife was, and how good she was at hiding things from me while I was on the road; quite the actress wouldn't you agree?

I ended up getting an apartment on Fremont Lake and missed my kids dearly every day I was away from them. I found out the affair had been going on for quite some time, it nearly destroyed our marriage, yet I still wanted the picture perfect family that I thought we had built together and was not ready to give that up for the sake of our daughters.

Her cowboy friend ended up marrying the other woman and I have never seen either of them again. Marlene, to this day, says she did no wrong. I tried to work on our relationship, but had very little trust in her. It was destroying our family and our children's life, because they knew something was going on.

Over time she was very convincing that nothing happened, that everyone in our small town in Hesperia, Michigan, was liars. I felt like I was back to when we first started dating, with a story being told to me about another guy that supposedly drugged her, and she didn't make it home after going out. I felt like I was living a bad episode of the "Twilight Zone".

It was like my wife never repented and I never truly forgave her affair, but we worked great together. The two of us. We were an awesome team and I forgave her for the sake of our girls.

Back to reality, I had to fly to Los Angeles, California, for a sales meeting, and the two managers took me out to a strip club. I felt very uncomfortable, but 'hey' my wife always said; "What's good for the goose is good for the gander," so I tagged along with them.

Both managers were both married; the one kept going into a back room with a dancer, soon after he came out, he said he needed to get going that his wife was going to be home.

We walked out to his car, the guy opened his trunk, pulled out a shirt, and changed it in the parking lot. I asked him, 'what are you doing that for?' He said, "So my wife doesn't smell perfume on me when I get home."

I thought, "Wow, what a piece of work." That was the first meeting I've ever been to in my life, that I never told my wife about something that happened on a trip, and the first time I've ever been in a strip club on a business trip.

When I got back home we were all business, fall was almost here, and it was our time to book all our orders for the spring season.

It was going to be very hectic on the road, with back-to-back meetings, and all the trade shows going on, one after another. My wife and I would be doing most of the traveling together with our kids when we could bring them.

I worked out of a home office, which made it very nice for our children. I never missed any baseball games or cheerleading; that was a true blessing.

One of the trips I'll never forget was when I went to Fort Worth, Texas, for a show and afterward almost all the vendors were flying to Reno, Nevada, to another show.

My flight out in the morning was for 10:00am on September 11th, 2001. But, I missed my girls so much, and wanted to go home and see them before I went on to Reno, so I changed my flight plans. I got on the red-eye on September 10th, 2001 at midnight for Chicago and then onto Muskegon, Michigan.

The next morning to my absolute 'HORROR,' as I awoke, the TV carried the news of the Twin Towers in New York, being hit by two airplanes. Knowing most of my friends were all on airplanes that morning, my heart sank. I was shocked at what was developing on the news.

It wasn't soon after all the airplanes were grounded. My phone started ringing. I had friends stranded all over the country. One friend Derrick, called me from LAX, his room over-looked the runway. He said, it looked like a ghost town out his window as he stared at the runways.

A few weeks later after flights resumed, there was a major Walmart line review in Dallas, Texas. Marlene was supposed to go to that one in the morning.

She had ten minutes to pack and make it to the airport in time for her flight. Going out the door she said; 'where do I stay.' I said, "Call me when you land in Dallas."

When Marlene got to Dallas, she called and asked, "where am I supposed to go for the meeting?" I said; "To the World Trade Center."

The phone went silent for a minute, she said; "What are you talking about?" I replied "They have a World Trade Center in Dallas, that's where the meeting is, you're booked in the Hotel next door," and I gave her the address.

Soon, I was back in the air again, but I didn't like all the new security rules. Just before 9/11, a pilot I knew in Muskegon, Michigan, let me take my daughters into the cockpit, before my flight. They were probably the last two girls in the new age of air travel to ever do that.

A lot of kids in my girl's class at school were frightened of flying, because of what happened in New York City on September 11th, 2001. So at the request of my daughters, I went to their school with them at Hesperia, and talked with their class about air travel. I was flying around a hundred thousand miles a year, and ever since I started traveling I had saved every flight ticket stub and hotel key card from my travels.

I have hundreds of them, and when I spoke with the children in class, on how safe air travel was, I passed the flight ticket stubs and hotel room cards around the room to the kids and they loved it!

Younger kids have a hard time with reality, and having no idea what was going on in the news; I truly felt it made a difference in their lives by taking the time to talk to them about flying at the time. By letting them know that I did not have a fear of air travel, especially after what had happened on September 11th, 2001, it did made a difference to them.

A few months later I was coming back into Chicago, Illinois, from Los Angeles, California; and we had a hard time landing, because of the weather, and the pilot came on, and said the rest of the flights that night were cancelled. I had Northwest Airlines, on my speed dial; so even before I got off the plane, I called customer service and they had me on the first flight in the morning.

As I was walking past the Northwest counter in the airport I saw everyone that had been on my plane standing in line to change their tickets. I thought, "Only if they knew, they could get on their cell phone, make the changes on the phone before they even got off the plane."

I also called the Hilton reservations from the plane and got one of the last rooms available in the hotel at the airport at Chicago. When I arrived at the hotel about thirty people in line trying to get rooms.

At the counter, the receptionist said, you got the last room, and a girl behind me freaked. As they were checking me in, she asked the receptionist if there was another hotel around, the girl at the counter said, she called everywhere, everything is booked because of the storm.

It was obvious with her accent that she wasn't from the U.S.A. She was very distraught and tired. I had a room with two queen beds, so I offered to let her stay in my room. She couldn't thank me enough.

Walking to the room, I found out she was from France, and was desperately trying to make it to Atlanta, Georgia, for a morning flight. I told her not to worry. When we got to the room, I called the airlines for her and made all the changes. She was on a Delta flight, transferring to KLM out of Atlanta.

When I called Delta it took longer, as her flights were International with connections, so I gave them all her information, and they said, they would call back in a few minutes. It took forty minutes, because they had to find a different International flight for her. After many calls I got her all set up to fly out in the morning.

Come to find out she was a model from Paris, France; she thought it was really cool that my daughter's name was Paris. We talked for a few minutes, but were both zonked out in no time. My wakeup call was for 5:00am.

I jumped up and grabbed my brief case. She woke up, and said; "Hang on a minute I have something for your daughters." She gave them both a signed photograph, then told me to tell my wife "hi", that she is a very lucky woman to have such a nice husband, thanked me again for my hospitality and fixing her flights.

I forgot about the photos and left them in my briefcase, I found them while getting ready for another meeting. The girls were at school and my wife was sleeping, because of my wife's jealousy I threw them away, which was sad because my girls would have liked them.

I'm pretty sure my wife would have used something as innocent as my helping someone in need, and turn it into an excuse to have another affair on me. I'm pretty positive of that so I had no choice, but to throw the photos away.

My gut feelings were coming more often now. So that was the second time I felt like something happened I could not tell my wife about. I was pretty sure her lack of conscious reality would have been twisted for her own personal use, as she could sense my lack of trust in her. It really bothered me that I couldn't be honest with her without distrust.

I was trying hard. My family is the most important thing to me. Any time another woman complimented me, my wife would get "big time", furious with jealous rage.

Once a friend of mine, named Sheri, told me she liked my shirt. After that, I could never find it, I asked my wife where my shirt was, she said; "I burnt it up." I thought, "Wow, why would my loving wife do that?"

Well looks like I can't pack that shirt for my next trip! I had to go to Houston, Texas, for my next meeting, and I was on a flight from Dallas. I had a while before my transfer. A guy sat by me in the lounge, and said, *"You were on the flight from Detroit."*

We started talking and he told me he was an air marshal, and said it was the third flight that he had profiled me on. They profile passengers who they determine can be called on in an emergency situation. Basically like—*"I've got your back!"*

One time, going to Los Angeles, California, from Detroit, Michigan, the ticket agent had seated me next to two guys obviously from the Middle East. When I sat down next to them they never said a word, looked around the plane or anything. When the stewardess asked them; if they wanted something to eat, they kept their heads down and said; "no, we're sleepy!" I think everyone on the plane profiled them when they got on the plane.

During the flight I had a lot on my mind. When we landed in Los Angeles, they just sat in their seat and waited for everyone to get off the plane. I'm sure traveling abroad for anyone from the Middle East was a nightmare because of what happened on September 11th, 2001, and was for them, as well. As humans we tend to take an act of wickedness and judge a whole culture for it.

I did my meeting in Los Angeles at Big 5 Sporting Goods and they ordered a truck load of merchandise. So besides the problems, I was having at home, my account executive back at the office was already on notice for messing up my accounts and costing me some major commissions.

Knowing this was a big order, and knowing my account executive was related to the owner, I half jokingly said, "If this guy in the office, (the owner's nephew) keeps losing my accounts, I'm going to have to go work for the competition."

The order was shipped a few weeks later, and I got a call from the Buyer, he wanted to know who the blank, blank, blank, it was that sent the purchase order to the buying office and not to the warehouse.

That would be the nephew, who never looked at the purchase order, and sent it to the first address he came across, which was the buying office. The higher ups at Big 5 Sporting Goods said; "Ship it back and cancel that order." If someone's that ignorant, as to ship a truck load of merchandise to our office instead of the warehouse—we don't need to do business with them.

National Accounts are hard enough to land, let alone to have someone who is in-house keep losing them due to their incompetence. Not to mention the cost of commission dollars they cost me and my family. It's not just getting the purchase orders; you have to have the right people in place to manage the accounts also, and deliver the goods.

After that, I had a serious conversation with the owner that if his nephew messed up any more of my accounts I'd have to leave and go to work for the competition, which he knew they already wanted to hire me. He understood my business decision to leave and still respected me.

My job was sky-rocketing in sales and now a competitor wanted to hire me to go to work for them. They made me an offer I couldn't refuse, my wife and I went down to meet the owners of a company in Fort Wayne, Indiana, to finalize the deal.

I had a simple marketing plan, I would double their sales every year, and I would work out of our home office, with a base pay plus one percent commission.

In the one-page contract, I also had a bonus clause that if I did eight million dollars the first year, they would give me thirty five thousand dollars bonus to purchase a Ranger Bass Boat, which was on my wish list. I already sold their product through a distributor, so I called those accounts first and turned them over factory direct with one phone call.

So right out the gate, I already landed two major accounts for my new employer. I have worked with every major retail account in the country, so I sat down at my home office, started to put my plan together of how I was going take the retail business away from the competition in an industry that was already cut-throat, vicious, and very competitive.

It was late fall when I started, the buying season for next spring was just getting started, so the timing was perfect. I wanted to land all the buying groups in the sporting goods industry. They were good for million dollar accounts and all I had on my mind was getting that bonus.

One of the first accounts I landed was NBS (Nation's Best Sports) out of Fort Worth, Texas. I attended their buying show in January, and on the first day of the show I ran into my Tournament sponsor friend; Nick, from Culprit. After the show we went to lunch together.

On the last night of the show, Nick wanted to take some buyer's to a bar called "Billy Bob's," in Fort Worth, that had bull riding inside the bar. That was way too cool. Afterwards, some of the cowboys knew me from fishing professionally and came over to our table.

They wanted me to take them all bass fishing. I said I can do that if you let me ride one of those bulls. We were supposed to fly out in the morning, so one guy said they would set it up for me to ride the bull and meet us in the morning at our hotel.

I called and changed my flight and everyone at the table started changing their flights also. Nick said, "I've got to see this; he's crazy but I didn't think that crazy!" I called my wife and told her I was going to ride the bull. Her response was, "What are you nuts! Who are you with?" I said, "Nick." She said, "Put him on the phone."

She tried to talk him out of letting me ride the bull and made Nick promise to call her when it was over. The next morning, we were all down in the lobby, and the cowboy came in and said he had bad news. The farmer with the bulls wouldn't allow it because of liability issues, if I should get hurt or killed. I felt let down at that point. I wanted to see how long I would have lasted on the back of a bull that had raging hormones.

That was one of the last times I would see Nick. Soon after, he passed away and I was deeply saddened for his family. Hopefully he doesn't forget me in heaven and that I brought a little excitement in his life.

For the next four years, my wife and I would go to Fort Worth for the NBS Show twice a year. The staff always hosted a vendor appreciation night and would have some kind of event where vendors could win prizes.

One night NBS had a casino night, my wife and I played roulette, something we've never played before. We actually got so lucky we broke the bank and ended up with all the chips.

Then you could turn the chips in for raffle tickets for prizes. My wife won this huge stainless steel tool cabinet. We won something at every NBS show we attended; usually always a VCR player or TV and the kids loved that.

Over the course of the year, I landed eight more major accounts, and earned my boat bonus from being a road warrior.

It's pretty simple landing major accounts, if you go into the product review meetings more prepared than your competition, and have your game plan together. There were very few accounts, that I didn't take a percentage of business away from the competition.

The key was, going in, being humble. Deliver what you promise in a timely fashion. My personality also helped out, my respect for the buyers; not to mention I had favor from the Lord over the competition.

You wouldn't imagine how many sales guys are so full of themselves, lay crap so deep on buyers, that when they leave their meeting the buyer just rolls his eyes! These are the guys that tell their bosses they've got the business, and never get a return phone call from the buyer.

You know the ones; they can write a very impressive sales report, filled with puff and smoke to the company owner, but never get the sale.

Other than having to attend the product review once a year, I also attended accounts' managers meetings, which usually involved a golf outing for vendors which was always fun. I've golfed some of the top courses throughout the United States.

Some of the accounts had their own tradeshows semi-annually, in the spring and fall; I loved this more than anything, because I could rack up sales for the entire year. That made it very easy to forecast production for each account.

From day one when my boss met me; he gave me a corporate credit card, company car allowance, and a lap top computer. He must have had confidence in me working out of a home office, because in three years of working for him he never once asked me what I was doing, how I did it, or ever questioned me about any travel expenses.

To put that kind of trust into a stranger, they must have had a lot of faith in me. Sometimes I wonder if I wasn't glowing at that meeting or that the Lord put their hearts at ease, they had total faith in my sales abilities.

I never thought about it, but they did put all their trust in me doubling their sales every year, could it be possible? I was blessed more than I could even comprehend, but not impossible, if you have help from a higher power, opening all the right doors for you, and protecting you on the road.

A typical year would start with traveling non-stop from January to March, with very little travel from April to August. That's the time I enjoyed immensely, because I got to watch all my daughters' softball games, which was very gratifying, making me the most blessed father in the world.

The meetings I had in the off months I always took the family. I made vacations out of them and our kids loved it. It just wasn't a vacation, if I didn't take our neighbor girl, Haley along. What a blessing she was for my daughters.

When September rolled around it was hustle time to November, for category reviews to land new product lines in the stores, steal shelf space from the competition, and make the competitors lives as miserable, as possible, when they seen me at meetings.

I'm sure that's what they thought, but I always enjoyed seeing the competition on the road and at tradeshows. You can learn a lot from the competition, if you pay attention.

Having accomplished my personal sales goals this year, it made having December off very pleasant around the house during the holidays. Shopping for the kids was always the best time of the year; this would be the best Christmas ever for my daughters, Eric, and Haley.

The upcoming year would take me to every state, except Hawaii, multiple times. I collected hundreds of shot glasses from airports. You could by a book, shot glass or spoon. I didn't need any spoons, so I collected shot glasses. I decided to write my own book, sell it in the airports, so all my competitors and friends that I've met over the years, can buy one!

I guess inside me, I'd known all along, that my perseverance would pay off, and someday my ship would come in. Loretta, bought me this little guy that said; "Someday my ship will come in!" I love the little guy. It still sets on my desk today.

With Christmas behind me, I had to start strategizing my game plan and get prepared for my busiest year ever, starting out with selling to the buying groups. I loved these shows the best, especially getting to see all my buyers' friends again.

Chapter Nine

MILLION DOLLAR DEAL BY NOON

My wife and I were off to Fort Worth, Texas, for the spring market of the NBS Show, which was held in January. I put together such an awesome "Hot Show" program, that by noon, I had buyers order over a million dollars worth of sales on one item. A sales girl named Angie, back at the office nick-named me; *"The Million Dollar Coon, by Noon!"* To this day that's never been done by any vendor, not even close.

Angie had a lot of talent and I could see in her that she was destined for big things. Years later she ended up moving to Los Angeles, and becoming a model. With her personality, one day she'll be a super model or a movie star. I could sense the light in her that she also was blessed, and all the right doors were going to open up for her in life.

Our next show was in Indianapolis, Indiana. Almost all the major cities I stayed in, I would always stay at the Hyatt.

After the show my wife and I went to the lounge, to meet some buyers and when they came in they yelled my name. Some guy sitting next to us asked me what my name was, and I told him. He said; "You're famous at the world hunt", that is where all the raccoon hunters go once a year, to see who has the best trained coon dogs.

They all wanted to hear my story on how I ran a deer down. Their favorite part was when I got a bow license the next day, and then Jimbo and I walked out past some duck hunters with our bow in the middle of the day. They told us good luck. We came back carrying this deer tied to a tree over our shoulders like *"Peter and the Wolf"*.

Every place we visited, there was always a new adventure around the corner. Shortly after, we had to go to New Orleans. You can't visit New Orleans, without going to Bourbon Street. We always stayed on or near Bourbon Street, close to all the action.

We made friends with a couple there, he was a bouncer at a local club, and she worked in the hotel. The man looked like Mr. Clean. They always took care of us when we brought buyers in for meetings. The first night in New Orleans, I even ran into Babe again, having dinner in the hotel restaurant.

New Orleans is an awesome town. I love the antique stores and we always went to the oyster bars. I also liked, Pat Obrien's for a hurricane, having our picture taken by the fountain with whomever we were entertaining that night. I could never figure out how my wife came home with all the beads when she went alone, and I never got any!

Going to Denver, Colorado, four or five times a year was always special as well, because I'd leave there, then drive to Sidney, Nebraska, to Cabela's and have dinner with a buyer friend of mine, named Jim. He had great hunting and fishing stories, but I'm pretty sure his kids caught the fish, letting dad take a picture with it.

It was always more enjoyable when my wife went on the road with me; *"we may not have it all together, but together we had it all!"* We were a force to be reckoned with working together at the shows and the competition knew that.

Denver was always a treat. You never knew what the weather was going to do, when the storms came over the mountains, you had better be at your destination and not get caught up in the storm. I've been stranded in Denver more times than I can count, but it's a great city to be stranded in. My sales manager, a good friend, Bob and I left Denver, for Sidney one afternoon and it snowed so hard that we couldn't even see the road signs trying to get out of town.

The worst part was it took us an hour to find the hotel we just left, and I don't think we made it two miles down the road and got lost. Now that's a snow storm!

My wife and I always enjoyed Minneapolis, Minnesota, on business trips. Staying at the Hyatt, we would take our buyers to Manning's for dinner. It's a place that has made the best steaks in town for over fifty years. It wasn't uncommon to have a thousand dollar dinner tab when we dined at Manning's with our buyers.

Another special restaurant that just my wife and I dined at was The Oceanaire Seafood Room. It's a retro supper club that serves the freshest seafood, with a very sophisticated relaxed and warm atmosphere for any couple. I'd always order my wife a bottle of "Chateau Lafite Rothschild." She'd always have the same comment, "It's the kind of wine you'd want to get naked for!" Minneapolis was always a lot of fun on our list of favorite cities to go to; it is a good place to spend time with buyers and friends.

I couldn't even begin to write about every city and town I was in. It would take a series of books to finish. Having been to every state except Hawaii, many times over, and each time was an adventure all in its own! I've never been to a city or town I didn't have a great time at. Life is what you make of it, I love to travel and see the country.

But when my best friend Rick and I would go to Alaska fishing; nothing compares to any other state. Ketchikan, Alaska, is on the edge of the world; you can't tell where, "Heaven starts or ends," the land is so majestic.

Even going through the inside passage it looks like the clouds are born in Alaska coming off the mountains. About the only word that can describe Alaska is "Heavenly", it is absolutely magnificent, truly God's country. One day, I hope to take my daughters there, on a cruise, and probably Haley too. I just pray to God, she doesn't say, 'This is the "bomb" on the cruise ship!'

If you're ever going to Alaska fishing and need a partner, take my friend Rick; you'll have no worries of him out fishing you, because the only thing he can catch is Salmon Sharks!

Leaving Alaska and flying to New York City for a meeting in Times Square; you step out of the Terminal in LaGuardia, look around and wonder if you made the right decision, leaving Heaven behind.

But hey, New York is New York, and I've never slept there in my life. How can you, there is way too much action going on to sleep. Usually it's checking into my room in Manhattan, a quick shower, and I'm out the door ready for adventure in the Big Apple. It's pretty nice having your meetings in Time Square, but it's rough being there with no sleep.

I would have to say Chicago ranks up there as one of my favorites. Maybe it's because I've been there a hundred times. I know where everything is at in the city, and that's where most of my accounts were. I do love staying at the Palmer House and dinning at Trader Vic's.

The best business trips are when I got to take my daughters along and our neighbor girl Haley; they are the most memorable ones. They've been with me on business meetings by land, sea, and air ~ which is pretty cool.

I don't think there is more of a blessing in the world, than being able to travel for work, and taking your family with you all the time while making it a vacation for them. I wouldn't want to give up that lifestyle for a million dollars.

Chapter Ten

BLESSINGS BEYOND BELIEF

My teams' sales efforts took us to new heights. Every year I doubled sales, but I had a lot of help from in-house people at the factory, that did their jobs to make it happen. This year I landed the company twenty nine major retail accounts, doing over fifty million dollars in sales, working out of a home office, over the last three years.

It kept me on the road constantly. Sometimes I'd be gone thirty days non-stop from meetings to tradeshows in the spring and fall. But if you want to dominate the market, you have to get aggressive, stay ahead of the competition, and have a better game plan than they do.

It doesn't take a rocket scientist to outsell your competition, you just have to sell smart, know everything about the competition and their sales managers. I knew my competitions personalities, their strengths and their weaknesses, more than they did. I knew every account they sold to, what items they were selling, and for the most part, had the competitor's sales history with the accounts, I knew what their programs were, before they did.

If you want to out sell the competition ~ you have to do your homework, develop a strategic game plan and take the business from them. Most sales people don't have a clue what they're doing, and they operate on what I call the "greed" sales mode.

They walk into the buyer's office with an arrogant attitude that they are going to sell their entire line to the buyer, replacing the competition with a sales pitch of deception a mile long that they lay on the buyer.

The key is to work with the buyer, supply him correct data and information that is going to make their stores successful in merchandising the category. I never, ever, would put down the competition. I would do the opposite. I would tell the buyer what items they should be carrying, (of the competitors) if he wasn't and why.

I would sell the category first, sell my competitors line to the buyer, and then the buyer would want to know what I had, and what SKU's (items) to carry from the line I was handling.

I don't know of anyone that would ever promote their competition, but there isn't a store in the world that's going to carry ONLY your line of merchandise, that's the GREED mentality of most sales people and company executives.

I taught this to a close friend of mine; a competitor and we worked well together. If either of us got wind of any category review coming up or new stores that were getting into our category line, we would tell each other.

Our sales strategy was simple; selling smart, he'd sell the products I wanted in the meeting and I'd sell his to the buyer. We were competitors promoting each other's lines; he and I always landed the accounts, secured the majority of the shelf space with our products over the other competition.

While our competition came into the meetings, with what little research they had done trying to sell their entire line, any reserved shelf space only allowed for one or two items at best. We dominated the category in almost all of the retail chain stores.

You have to remember if the stores aren't successful with the category they will drop it! You have to promote or at least acknowledge a few of your competitors top selling SKU's (items) if you want to see those stores survive in today's economy.

Some buyer's had so much respect for me that when they opened new stores, they didn't even call the competition, they would come to me with their price lists, and ask me what items I should carry in their stores. I'd show the buyer what to carry, and how many to order. Guess who got the biggest order every time, without even making a sales pitch!

What I Learned Under the Sun, is to have your sales double every year, you have to work with your buyers and the competition. It wasn't by accident that I did over fifty million dollars in sales in three years in the most competitive, cut throat industry, I've ever been in. It wasn't by accident that I doubled the owner's sales every year; I also worked with a lot of great people behind the scenes, without them it wouldn't have been possible.

What I Learned Under the Sun, is it's all about "honesty", being "humble", and that's how you make sales under the sun!

I had so many meetings and shows going on, that sometimes it was a challenge to find someone to fill-in for me with multiple shows going on at the same time of the year. I was on the road constantly, sometimes, my wife would have to fly to a show or do a meeting for me.

Once she went to Salt Lake City, Utah, a day that I'll never forget. Marlene was leaving the meeting, while walking across a busy intersection when the light turned red, she crossed in front of a big truck, a car ran the red light and blew by her, coming within inches of running her over. Marlene said, it was too close for comfort, it really shook her up!

The Lord was with us that day, and protected her. That's the kind of things you take for granted about your spouse; my God what would you do if something happened to your wife?

This would be our busiest year yet, logging in over a hundred thousand air miles. I couldn't even begin to count how many trips my wife and I went on together. It was definitely a year of Blessings.

My most memorable tradeshow was when I took my daughter Paris to Cincinnati, Ohio, with me. The entire buyer's group knew my kids. At the show one buyer friend of mine named Linda, came into our booth, and took Paris around with her on the show floor to buy products for her store.

Paris was all dressed up and looked like a professional little lady, just having the time of her life. She was definitely a "Big Shot" at the show. Everyone loved her dearly. I was never so proud of my daughter in my life. That was by far the best show I've ever done, not for sales but to be with my daughter.

One of the other trips my daughters loved to go on, was when I had to go to Appleton, Wisconsin, for meetings. We always took the car ferry out of Ludington, Michigan, to Manitowoc, Wisconsin. We did this at least four times a year.

I always took our neighbor girl Haley, who became part of our traveling family. Marlene's son Eric who was older, stayed home most of the time because he didn't want to travel with his sisters.

Sometimes we would drive around Lake Michigan coming back, and always stay in Mackinac City, Michigan, and I'd take the girls over to Mackinac Island. One time we were sitting in a restaurant on the Island eating, the girls were in the front window drinking kiddy cocktails, and of all people their teacher walks by and sees them. They laughed about that all day. When we left there, we rented a horse and buggy driver and toured the Island.

Life was great, especially with the girls. They loved to travel with their dad on the road. I had a meeting in Florida, and took everyone to Disney World to a meeting with me. My boss said it was alright to take a week off after the meeting, so I could take my daughters with me.

The meeting was in January, so for Christmas presents, everyone got new luggage and airplane tickets to Disney World. We were becoming quite the jet setting family. Marlene, Eric, Paris, Skyler, and Haley, could hardly stand it waiting for January to get here.

    I don't even think, it was the day after Christmas, and all three girls had their luggage packed and ready to go to Florida. Myself, I still had a ton of work to do, getting ready for my busiest season ever. When I got back from Florida, I would have to leave the next day to another show and I would be gone off-and-on for three months straight, working. I needed all my programs completed, schedules done for each show coming up, who was going with me, and what product samples needed to be sent where; before I could even think about packing for Disney World.

    We are all packed and heading to the airport for Florida. I'm telling the girls, *"Whatever you do; don't say the word "Bomb" on the airplane."* (This was because of new flying rules due to September 11th, 2001 bombing of the Twin Towers in New York City.) I had sandwiches I bought in the airport for the girls. We no more got into the air and Haley yells out; *"This sandwich is the bomb!"* I said; *"Haley, you can't say bomb on the airplane."* It was way too hilarious. That girl cracks me up!

    We landed in Florida, and the kids we're excited, big time. We got our shuttle van loaded up and headed to the Disney Resort. We rented a cabin for the week and a golf cart to get around in during our stay.

    I think they liked riding around in the golf cart just as much as everything else there. We'd take the golf cart to a boat and then take a boat to Disneyland. Some of the other parks we had to take a bus and every day it seemed like we got back just in time to catch dinner before the restaurant would close.

    One day at Disney World we ate lunch at the Castle and the kids loved that. My girls we're definitely princesses of the day. I don't think we got to go on all the rides but we had a blast. The blessing for me was

I got to video the entire trip for the girl, just seeing how happy they were, was priceless!

At the end of the day the girls loved getting back to the cabin because the maid would always leave extra towels in the bedroom on their beds in the shape of different animals. That was one vacation all of us hated to see end, but we had to get back home for another road trip.

After getting back home from many grueling months on the road, I remembered, having lunch at the Castle, I haven't got my wife her castle yet, and it was time to find her one. I made so many sales over the last six months since Disney World, which my boss said, he would help us out getting our home.

We were in the grocery store and saw this advertisement for a really cool house on the river with its' own island. So we went and looked at it, the girls fell in love with it. With the help of my boss, giving me an advance towards my commission due, I bought the house, and we moved into the house in July.

The house was a three bedroom ranch right on the river. The Island that was part of the property had two huge willow trees on each end of it and had a bridge wide enough for me to ride my riding lawnmower over to mow.

In the center of the Island we had a fire pit. The girls loved to have bon fires out there. The river itself was very shallow and when the Salmon ran up the river to spawn in the fall, you could hear and see them coming up the river before they even got to our island.

My boss owed me two hundred thousand dollars in commissions, so he loaned me the money to get the house until they could get my commissions caught up. It would also be a perfect place to hold business meetings for customers and entertain them.

The next show I was at, in the fall, there was a kayak manufacturer, so I bought their entire booth of seven kayaks. I had them all shipped by UPS, to my home, and when the driver pulled in, my girls were at school. I unloaded the kayaks and had them all lying in the driveway.

When Paris, Skyler and Haley got home from school they went crazy seeing all those kayaks lined up. When they jumped off the school bus and came running up the driveway they had the biggest smiles in the world on their faces.

My first rule was they couldn't use them on the river until they could learn to paddle upstream! Every day, I took Paris, Skyler and Haley kayaking about a mile downstream, taught them to read the river currents, and paddle back up-stream. Paris and Haley caught on fast, but it took Skyler a little longer. She came around in a matter of weeks, and was buzzing up and down the river like it was nothing.

One weekend we were way downstream, turned around, started paddling up, and every time we saw people in canoes they would all say, "You're going the wrong way." One time a guy I knew said, *"What, are you training your girls to be in the Olympics, Kyle?"* They were pretty much experts on the river by now and none of their friends could do it.

Fall rolled around, and then the fun really started with the salmon run! My girls were like the *"Queen's of the River"*. The fish didn't have a chance when they came past the island. Especially Paris; she caught so many fish we lost count.

My buyer's would come in, Paris was their guide, she taught them all how to fish, what to use, and where to cast. Every time they hooked into one, Paris would jump in the river in her hip boots and net the fish for my buyers. My buyer's weren't just business associates; they were my friends of many years.

I think in the fall there was a fire nonstop day and night on the Island when the fish were in the river. My office was in a closed-in-porch, that over-looked the river and every time a fish came up the river, my girls would scream past me running for their fishing poles to see who could catch it first. I had the best office location in the world by far.

I had the smoker going constantly, smoking salmon.

My buyers would love it; they'd call for something, start talking fishing, and want to know if the salmon are in yet. My buddy Jim from Cabela's called, my wife answered my cell phone, and she told him just a minute. He said; "he's got a fish on doesn't he!"

It's pretty hard talking to the buyer with a cell phone in one hand while a twenty pound salmon is on the other end of your rod in your other hand and is screaming down the river.

My daughter Paris entered a fishing contest. I came home from a meeting one day, walked into my office; Paris is standing on the island, yelling, *"Dad, I got one!"* I dropped my briefcase, ran to the island, grabbed a net, jumped in the water with my suit on and dress shoes to net her fish. It was so big, I had to go a hundred yards downstream to net it.

Paris was persistent; she was in a big fish contest for the local Salmon festival, in Hesperia, Michigan. With that salmon, she ended up taking third place in the tournament two years running. That's my 'girl', out-fishing all those guys!

When the fall colors start turning, that's when the fish start migrating upstream by the thousands, and fall is the best time of the year for the whole family.

We would always take drives to see the autumn colors, look for mushrooms, or my wife and I would just walk down a two track holding hands. Our girls loved it also, but I had to keep a close eye on Paris, because she'd like to take off and adventure in the woods by herself. My little girl had no fear in the woods; I wonder who she gets that from?

The leaves were off the trees and deer season was about to open. We had a client come in to go deer hunting. On opening day, I shot a huge buck and it dropped in a guy's field. I watched some guys come up in a truck and load my deer up, I shot. My wife comes running over to me and says some idiots are stealing your deer!

I told her it's no big deal. They must need it worse than I do. The Lord will bring me another one. She walked away mad and about half hour later two deer come running underneath my stand and I got them both.

When Marlene heard me shoot, she came, running back to my stand amazed that I got two more deer. I had no doubts the Lord would provide for me if I allowed them guys to steal my deer.

Lucky for them, the Lord put it on my heart to let them have the deer and I allowed them to get away with it! It was, their lucky day.

Later in the season when the snow was on the ground, a friend called me to go help him track his deer. I met him and we took off for the woods. When we found the deer, as I bent over to clean it, I heard a hiss sound and felt my hair move.

Then a gun shot rang out. I turned and looked and you could see in the snow where the bullet streaked across the ground behind me. About a few second later a deer was flying buy in the thick brush, I dove for my gun and got one shot off as it was disappearing into the thicket.

I told my buddy when we get done we'll have to come back and get my deer! He said, *"What deer you didn't get him, you missed!"* I told him to walk over there and see, he came walking back with a big smile and said, "What a nice four point you got, you're the luckiest guy I know!"

Was it luck? No. I just had a bullet whiz by my head so close that it moved my hair. I guarantee you it wasn't luck! If I wouldn't have felt it and seen the track of the bullet in the snow, which would have been just another time in my life the Lord has protected me and I wouldn't of known it.

Very few people realize that they have many instances in their lives they were protected by guardian angels or a Higher Power, and had no clue their lives were ever in danger. I'm just a normal guy. I couldn't even imagine how many times the Lord has protected me from certain death unbeknown to me.

Fall slowly slipped away, and another Christmas was here. Hard to believe, a year has already passed since Disney World. Around our house it was family tradition to let the girls open a present on Christmas Eve and I always made it a special night for my wife.

When the kids went to bed, I always would have that special gift for her and we would always have a candle light dinner with Lobster and shrimp. I always looked forward to Christmas Eve to spend that special moment with my wife and patiently wait for my Angels to fall fast asleep so I could put their presents under the tree.

My biggest challenge at Christmas time, was trying to get my wife under the mistletoe; sometimes she was hard to catch or was she just was playing hard to catch?

We've been in our new house now for six months. Our family had a lot to be thankful for. It was truly a blessed year for our family and I thanked God for that.

My boss was in the process of selling his company for what some of his family told me was well over a hundred million dollars. With the new year on us we we're kicking back waiting for that huge commission check I had earned.

Just prior to the sales of the company the bosses son called me and said; "Kyle, the sale of our Company won't go through unless you can make it happen". I said; "What's wrong?" he told me that, "none of the buyer's will accept any calls from the investor buying their company, and I need you to call him, and get him on a conference call with all your buyers."

Within two days I had the task completed; the owners' son called, thanked me, and then told me after the deal went through; "I was going to be very happy". My wife and I were ecstatic, yet we had no idea what our boss's son was going to do for us now that the Company was sold.

Chapter Eleven

SATAN AT MY FRONT DOOR

No one ever plans on sin, but when Satan's at your front door you only have two options; turn him away or invite him into your life! What was about to develop was beyond my comprehension and I wouldn't of believed it, in a million years.

It's been over six months since my boss and his son sold their business and they still had not paid me the monies they owed me in commissions, yet alone whatever the son, talked of that "I would be very happy", when the company sold.

This was bugging the heck out of me and it was driving my wife crazy, things were becoming strained in the house again.

My wife went back to spending more time going to the bar partying, like she did before we were married. Then one night, decided under the influence, to bring home two male bartenders to our new home. I woke up and she was sitting in the middle of them on the couch in our living room making out with one of them. I threw the drunks out of the house and my wife went with them.

I learned she just allowed Satan into her life of lust. Sex is the battlefield of marriage and Satan uses the weapon of lust, day-in and day-out in everyone's marriages.

She comes home about three in the afternoon, full of apologies, and promises she'll make it up to me. I'm thinking; "How can you make it up to me for committing adultery with our children sleeping right in the house." Satan was at my front door and my wife invited him in. This was the start of a major downward spiral in my family's life.

Marlene was hanging around a new friend, from the bar who now was her best friend. Her son Eric couldn't even stand her around the house. The more Marlene and her friend drank, the mouthier they both became with our daughters in their presence. I'd always tell the both of them to leave, and under the influence of alcohol, my wife's new friend would always, say; "You've never done anything for your girls, you're bi-polar." And I'm thinking, "I'm bi-polar?" "Who's taking the crazy pills?"

Day-in and day-out, this woman would say negative comments to my girls like that. It got to be like an old record. The police said; I couldn't have her removed from the house because she was a guest of my wife's. It's actually insane that a mother would let a person around her daughters that talked trash like that.

Marlene was on a spiral spin and was taking her whole family down with her. I was literally devastated by her actions and was without comprehension. What the heck was going on in her life? She turned into someone no one liked as a person, except for her male bar friends; most of the women in town hated her for what she was doing.

That hurt me a lot when people talked about her in the bar, and it bothered Eric for a long time hearing guys talk about, being with his mom.

I didn't believe a lot of what I heard, because I knew most of it was lies, and most of her male bar friends wanted her divorced. Everyone else in town was just as disgusted with her at this point. We lived in a very small town on the edge of the world, called; Hesperia, Michigan.

I could see the damage she was causing our children and Marlene's heart was so hardened, she had no idea what she was doing to our girls. I was beyond myself, that a mother could do this. The woman turned so deep into sin, that she had no clue what she was becoming and the path of destruction she left behind was for eternity and she called it; "a new age."

I could not have imagined, that turning from God, would have such destructiveness and deadly consequences. She made the turn to evil and wickedness.

As a loving husband, I was seeing the devastation of that type of lifestyle, and the effect it was having on my daughters, it was killing them and destroying their mother in the process. Marlene was on a collision course, which spelled, "disaster" for our happy family.

An enemy will always point to a problem in your life and never offer a solution. They will feed your addiction and never offer the recovery. They will tear you and your family down rather than build you up. They feed on your mistakes, problems or hurts and wait in the dark like little wolves.

I was having a hard time dealing with my wife and my employer who was not paying what he owed me in travel expenses and/or commissions, even after he sold his company, which I helped to facilitate, by the request of his son.

After the sales of the company I met with the new CEO, and he introduced me to the new VP of Sales (my new boss) the first words out of his mouth to me were; *"I don't like anything about you, from this moment on you are not to make any more sales calls."*

I knew in an instant the new company was going to lose most of their business with this arrogant guy in charge. My buyers had nicknamed him *"jackass"*, and for good reason.

When the new company took over, they brought in new people and replaced all of the executive positions with the titles of VP's and I assure you it fit all their personality to a tee! They were the most arrogant people I've ever met in my life.

One VP they had, I was forced to take to a meeting with me because she had a title of VP and smarter than me!

Well we went to a K-mart meeting, she walked into the meeting and told the buyers, who were friends of mine; "that they didn't know how to do their jobs and she's here to teach them how". We all looked at each other, with the same thought I'm sure; *"Are you kidding me!"*

Remember what I told you about what I call the "greed" sales mode. This is a perfect example; the new VP that has no sales experience, no relationship with the buyer and knows nothing about the Account or the competition. She (VP) walks into a major meeting and tells the buyers; *"they don't know how to do their jobs."* She is here to teach them and they should replace all their suppliers, because she said so.

I can't even tell you what the buyers said; when he called me on my cell phone after the meeting with this woman. It was a few months later the new company fired the woman ~ wow, imagine that!

My new boss the *"jackass"* had me go to all my accounts with him and introduce him to the buyers. That was very interesting, because the new way of doing business was you had to give a report on the meeting.

When I read this guy's reports he e-mailed to me; I'm thinking to myself, what planet did this guy come from, I was in that meeting and nothing in his report resembles what was discussed in the meeting.

He's the type of sales guy that gives a puff and smoke sales report to the owner's of the company and never gets the purchase orders. The way I did a report, before the new owners took over; was, I went to the meeting and came back to the office with a purchase order, simple as that; here's my report.

I never wrote a report in my life at this company, my strategy was, I'll give you an order and you make sure you can produce and ship on time. Guess what, we never missed a deadline because the company knew exactly how much inventory they had to produce to fulfill my purchase orders and I doubled sales every year.

After my contract expired, I got a call to come to their new office and the new CEO and VP told me I was fired; *"for lack of sales"*, like, I didn't see that coming. Today they both are probably sitting behind a desk, to see who can write the best report to the new owner, on how much the company is going to make and how much they've saved by cutting corners.

I got an e-mail from a friend at the company, telling me their first year after they fired me their sales were down forty four percent. I was not surprised a bit. The new CEO told me he wanted ten "Kyle's" and to this day he still hasn't found one.

Things went from worse to real bad; I went to a competitor for a job interview in Dallas, Texas. When I came home my wife moved another family into our house. Some hippy cousin of hers, that always mooches off the family. Did that ever throw a spin in our household!

Marlene's son was graduating in a month and now we have her cousins living with us. They pretty much stayed out of my way and never communicated with me. They spent their evenings sitting outside on the patio partying, overlooking the river or left and went bar hopping.

Eric's graduation was a week away and my wife basically planned everything for the party with her cousins and kept me in the dark. I felt like an outsider in my own home.

The weekend arrived and they started the night before getting ready and had a Hawaiian Pig Roast. My wife, as great as she is, decorated the garage very nice.

Everything was draped in white including the tables out back by the river. She even had the island decorated; it looked like we were having a fancy wedding.

I pretty much did what I was told; I didn't have any say-so in her son's graduation. That bothered me a lot, it was all about impressing her cousins and I had no use for them.

The most important thing was that Eric had a great party and enjoyed the day because it was all about him. I think he was very happy with his graduation party. The guests were overwhelmed on the great job my wife did.

It wasn't too long after the party Marlene's cousins were taking her out to the bars again.

I came home one night from a meeting and the cousin's wife told me when I walked in the door that she was going to own my house under *"squatters rights"* as she was putting her dishes in my cupboards.

She had a pile of her dishes on the counter and she was putting them away, I flung them in the garbage and I told her, to get her; *"squatter's butt"* out of my house and take her crap with her! "Squatters rights", sort of brought the craziness to a head when I heard that.

The low-life called the police, to have me removed out of my home and they told her; "that she had to leave, that they weren't welcome." I finally stuck up for my family and got the squatters out!

My wife got irrate because I threw them out of the house and she woke up my daughters and told them, "your daddy is kicking us out of the house, we have to move girls."

Here are two angels being pulled out of their beds, Told their dad is kicking them out of their home, (their mom is forcing them to leave), and that he is making them leave, so they walked out the door with the squatters.

Marlene moved her cousins into our town house, and the next day came back with the squatters and started moving everything out. I was glad to see them go, but felt sorry for our girls being caught up in her madness, the sadness in their eye's was more than I could handle.

All this time, I've been in a marriage that's been nothing but lies and deception. What do they call that; "Blinded by love?" Holy smokes; now I know why you wait on the Lord to bring you a Proverbs 31 woman to marry.

A few months later, I let my wife move back in for the sake of my daughters. We tried to move on, and neither one of us ever talked about any of the problems in our marriage.

She wanted nothing to do with it because like she always states; "It's not true honey. I would never do that." Even though everyone else in the community told me a different story, Marlene always convinced me to believe her.

She let the squatters stay in our townhouse for six more months before they finally moved out.

With all this craziness going on, I'm still having the issue of my boss never paying me my commission; this made monumental problems in our marriage. I could only imagine if my boss would have been a man of his word and paid me, where we would have been at today.

My wife didn't just wake up and say; I'm going to become a drunk today, getting stiffed out of my commissions took a major toll on her.

Since my boss sold his company, I had to work with the new owner on trying to get paid my commission. They drug this out so long that I had to finally hire a lawyer to file a wage claim against them.

This angered my old boss so he filed papers in court to have us evicted out of our home on a quick claim deed one week before Christmas. Go figure! You make the guy over fifty million dollars in sales in three years; doubling his sales each year, and this is the thanks we get.

Then his son tells you the sales of his company won't go through unless you can make it happen. So you use all your influence and make the deal go through. They get their money and get the attitude; "oh, well too bad" we've got our money! That's where the deadly sin of greed comes into play.

The profit bonus I was promised, according to the son, for making the sales go through, for over a hundred million dollars, would have made my family very happy. Well, a year later, we got a check for a thousand dollars bonus, after he evicted us from our home for owing us over two hundred thousand dollars in commissions. This is a man that struts around like a peacock, claiming to be a Christian, who had us evicted on Christmas Eve.

He and his son knew I was owed the money, that's why he gave me the money in the first place to buy the house. The dad is the one who had the last say. Since he sold his company, he received his money, and he had his own family to take care of.

Then to evict us on Christmas Eve—pretty much sent me and my wife over the edge! If he was a Christian man he would have written a check and made it right with my family; he wouldn't be on easy street without my influence. The man didn't see it that way; he was so FULL of PRIDE. A close relative said, "The dad, felt bad", but it was out of their hands, since they sold the company. Out of his hands, that's funny, he hired me, I honored my end of the deal, double his sales every year, but when the company sold, it was out of his hands.

We ran into the son at the Shot show and we invited him out to dinner to try and find out what was going on with his dad not paying me.

After the show he sent us a message; Kyle and Marlene, "I wasn't trying to be rude at the Shot Show, but a combination of being very busy and feeling awkward about all the things I have put you through lately lead me to believe that the invitation to dinner wasn't on the top of the list for either of us. Sorry! Never is it my goal to burn bridges and hopefully I haven't, but I understand if I have, best of luck in the future."

That message made the both of us even madder that they wouldn't pay us and felt awkward about stiffing us, a major slap in the face to me, my wife and our innocent children. The son should of just said; "It's sucks, to be you", my daddy and I got our money!

Thank Goodness my boss has his new Lear jet airplane; he'll be able to land it on God's runway on judgment day. It amazes me that some people that claim to be a Christian are the ones that will deceive you the most, then stiff you in the name of "greed".

They pretend to be Christians, yet they still are so full of pride and until they learn the secret under the sun they will never figure it out. The secret is in your heart, if you don't have pure love in your heart you have no soul; no matter how much you try to justify your actions in your mind. "Thou shall not kill." What their "greed" did to my family was murder, in God's eyes. "Thou shall not kill", just doesn't mean murdering someone at the hands of a weapon. Your actions in life can be just as deadly as a murder weapon, just a slower death.

I have a feeling the only reason my wife moved back in was because she heard I filed a wage claim against my boss and for the sake of my daughters I took her back. Then we started working together again on the wage claim. I worked for an out-of-state company so under law they were required to pay three times damages on wages and I think that was the attraction to my wife.

We met the lawyer and submitted our evidence. It was very clear I made the sales and was owed the money, so he took my case on.

The out-of-state lawyer I hired filed my wage claim that would become a year process in discovery.

You think the man would have done what was right in his heart and pay me, we proved in discovery that the man owed me the money and he still refused to pay me still owing me forty four thousand dollars in travel expense reimbursements. I guess he figured since he was a multi-millionaire he could use his team of lawyers to financially break me to win the case.

He probably spent more on lawyers than if he would have just paid me what he owed me, amazing what greed can do to some people. We proved he owed me, but when it would come to writing that check, it was just too hard to let go of that money now that he sold his company.

After spending what seemed like months of putting all the evidence together it was finally my day in court.

On my first day in court my boss had five lawyers present and filed multiple counter claims basically turning me from a plaintiff to a defendant and requesting almost impossible information for more discovery documents, trying to prolong the case in court for years, like I said; a slow painful death on my family.

They submitted all my corporate credit card statements for three years, as part of their defense was I had to explain three years of travel. When that came in the mail my wife sat down and spent a month going over each statement.

Marlene has been with me to virtually every city I've been to, so she knew where I always stayed and where I took buyers out when I entertained them.

My court process took me about a year to compile about three huge binders of evidence for the discovery process. It literally, became a full time job.

I was trying to land another sales and marketing job and getting shot down everywhere I went. Come to find out, my new boss, the "jackass" at the new company, was telling potential employers that, he had to fire me for lack of sales ability.

I took this as a compliment that the new owners had that much fear with me as a competitor. What comes around goes around, I think it was within a year they already replaced most of the so called experts they hired to do my job.

Still unable to find work, my wife was having a lot of resentment towards me. I'm not sure if it was because of the economy and I couldn't land a job or it was my boss stiffing me for my commissions and evicting us out of our home just before Christmas.

The fact was, she brought sin into our home and the Lord literally slammed the doors shut on our family. Door after door was closing and that's a scary feeling when you're living it. But you have to keep the Faith and wait patiently for God to open the right doors in your life.

The lawyer ended up spending all his time trying to fight the counter-claim. He ended up charging us tens of thousands of dollars and we had to drop him because we ran out of money. So I had to find another law firm to handle my case.

It's pretty pathetic that you work so hard for a company and in the end the owners stiff you and have no regrets doing it. That's not an uncommon practice with manufacturers; I know many good men and woman that were stiffed out of their commission because the owner couldn't write that check because it was too large.

It's all about greed. Manufacturers want you to get them into all the chain stores with their products, making them millions of dollars overnight. Then the retailer pays the company and when it comes time for the owner to write that check for sales commissions, is when greed sets in.

Owners have good intentions, but find it to difficult to write a six figure check to a sales person after he's got his money. I don't think there are too many top sales people in the world that can't relate to this statement, I know everyone I've dealt with has been there and done that.

Soon after getting nothing for my commission, my wife started working in a bar and partying with some "new" friends. One night her friend called at three in the morning and wanted to talk to my wife. I said; *"She's not here!"* She said; "I know she's there, because she left my house a long time ago." I hung up on her.

About a half hour later, a truck rides by the house really slow and stops in the church parking lot just past our house. I'm watching my wife out of the front window of our house. Marlene gets out of the truck of a male bartender "friend" she works with, and staggers home down the road.

Can you imagine? Someone's out committing adultery, which is denied and ends the night in the church parking lot before you go home to your spouse?

She walks in the house just smashed on her butt and walks up stairs like it's no big deal. A few months later she started working at another sleazy bar outside of town. This caused all kinds of problems in our marriage.

It wasn't long, she was going to the bar without her wedding ring on, dressing provocative, and telling me and the kids she's; "Just doing her job and the guys wouldn't tip her unless she dresses like that."

Pretty soon she was going to work earlier and coming home later and later. I started going into the bar and almost every time she'd be sitting with the same old man that thinks he's a cowboy called; Charlie. I asked her about him, why he's always hanging around. She said; "It's not what you think honey, we're just friends!"

My mind and gut is telling me "Oh, he just happens to be with you every time I walk in the bar." This was really starting to tick me off and rumors in town are she's been having an affair with the guy, for quite some time. She would spend two hours getting ready for work; my wife's whole life was revolved around the bar.

Marlene would get home at 3:00am to 4:00am in the morning, I'd get the girls up make them breakfast and drive them each day to school while my wife slept until about noon. Marlene would get up go to the fridge, grab a beer and start getting ready for work. Our girls would get home about 3:30pm from school and Marlene would have enough time to ask them how nice does mom look and out the door she went into the night.

This went on seven nights a week. I finally told her I've had enough. She needs to quit the bar, start staying home and become a mother to our girls. It's time to act like someone, and quit running to the bars every night.

I'll never forget that day; she walked out the door, looked back in her fur coat with her hair all done up, laughed and flipped me the bird as she walked by the window and left me home to make Thanksgiving dinner for her family.

Chapter Twelve

THE TURNING POINT—DIVORCE

I spent all night preparing a beautiful Thanksgiving dinner. The next day my wife got up at noon, her parents will be here in an hour.

She drops the "Big" bomb on me as I'm checking the turkey; "I want a divorce, I want to see someone." Just more doors closing on me. Right about this time I'm not feeling very thankful and I'm having serious issues with the Proverbs 7 Woman I married.

Now I've got this going on, I'm trying to find a new law firm to take my case with absolute chaos around the house. I had all I could do to make up another set of discovery binders for the wage claim, and send them to another law firm to review before Christmas. This was the surprise I had for my wife for a Christmas present.

Like, I didn't see that coming. This "Charlie" guy has been chasing her for a year. It took that old man that long to seduce her. You don't want to believe your wife is committing adultery on you, so you truly have eyes but you can't see!

Even though the joke in the bar for the past six months was her affair, everyone was telling me; *"She's a devil woman."* Sadly over the course of the next year that is exactly what she became.

I went to the bar to talk with her, there is Charlie sitting with her, he gets up and leaves. I walk in and say "Marlene, we've got two girls you need to think about, this has to end." She says, *"I don't care about that, walk away!"* That infamous line, *"walk away."* Now I remember where she got it; from that millionaire that wanted me to; "*walk away*" back at the bed-and-breakfast!

At another bar she works at, she has a new friend who is a counselor by day and barmaid by night. My wife says her friend the counselor is giving her advice and she wants a divorce.

I'm thinking, great, your taking marriage advice from a barmaid, that's had multiple divorces and living a life of sin! That's like going to a dentist and asking him for advice on what's wrong with your brain.

Our house was in shambles, it was getting close to Christmas again. I just knew with her affair going on; it wasn't going to be a very pleasant Christmas for anyone in our household, including my girls. I told my wife we need to go get at least a few more gifts for the girls.

So we went to the mall. Marlene walks into Victoria Secrets store and spent our last three hundred dollars on lingerie; she said, she needed it for New Years. Something she has never bought, in sixteen years of our marriage! I pretty much knew it wasn't for me!

I am livid. Are you kidding me? We're not going to buy anything for the girls and you're only worried about yourself, what you're going to wear on New Years, "wow", talk about lost in sin!

The next day when she got up at noon I tried to talk with her again, more like pleaded with her to go with me and talk to a Christian marriage counselor. And she wanted nothing to do with it saying; "that I love my life, I love everything about the bar." Marlene had no desire to leave that lifestyle!

You truly can't talk to anyone under the influence. They are not in their right mind. Partying on a daily basis they have no clue about reality. My wife was escaping life and using prescribed drugs to do it, she wanted no help.

Marlene, called the prescription drugs; her "I don't care pills", a drug prescribed by a doctor to help with depression or chemical imbalance. My wife was escaping reality, I observed a very dangerous addicted behavior and she wanted no help.

If you took the bar out of our marriage, we wouldn't be getting divorced and she knows this! We had a great marriage, very few ups and downs, I tried making things work, our only issues was the bar, if she wasn't in the bar, we did everything together, played games alone and truly enjoyed each other.

We had a few problems in our marriage, what one doesn't? Her affair in the bar killed our marriage. Every argument or disagreement we had has been over one thing; *"the bar"*.

My Family's Christmas party was tomorrow and my wife said she wasn't going. She had to meet her friend at the bar early, and wouldn't have time to make it back! Not to mention the hang up call's I've been getting the last few months. So Paris, Skyler and I went alone. That pretty much, killed the Christmas Spirit for all of us.

We got home and my wife was just leaving. Her son came home for the weekend. I went to the Legion to see what my wife was up to. A guy came up to me and said; "I just saw your wife at the other bar, and she was all over me!"

I had a couple of friends there who saw I was very upset and I left with them to cool down. They dropped me back at the Legion, where I left my truck; I had a mile to go down the road when a Hesperia police officer pulled me over by my house, because, I had a smashed out headlight. I told him my light was intact when I arrived at the Legion earlier in the night. I usually don't have to encircle my vehicle after parking in a lot where I arrived and everything on my car was in working order.

Like the nightmare from fifteen years ago he took me to jail for impaired driving, and I demanded a blood test at the hospital because I didn't drink that much. I couldn't get a hold of my wife all night. The next night she finally answers the phone and I ask her to come and bail me out, she says, *"Sucks to be you!"* again "are *you kidding me*?"

I can't imagine anyone that wouldn't stand by their spouse's side. Isn't that the whole point of marriage; becoming one and knowing you will always have someone in your world you can count on no matter what?

I had to call my sister to come bail me out. I found out later that a friend "Sheri" offered to give my wife the money to get me out and she said, "Screw that." That didn't surprise me that Sheri came to my rescue. In my eyes, she's the one person I've felt love within a person as if she was the Proverbs 31 woman.

My sister and brother-in-law came and bailed me out and gave me a ride home. My wife had already changed the locks on the house so I couldn't get in. I basically had the clothes on my back. They gave me a ride to my mom's house.

At the time I didn't realize it, but my loving wife filed a PPO (Personal Protection Order) on me so I couldn't come near the house. That was just the most, wicked game of deceit that I could ever comprehend anyone doing to a loved one at Christmas time.

Then, to top that off, Marlene had my step son Eric serve me the papers. I was pretty blown away by the whole thing. I asked Eric, "have you read this" and he put his head down and said; "yes" I couldn't believe what I was reading. More evil and wickedness beyond comprehension, so evil I started crying, Eric hugged me and said; *"you knew what she was when you married her"* then told me bye and left. A pretty strong statement from her son!

I guess what hurt me the most is the contents of the PPO. Marlene stated, in the PPO that; "I dress in black, girls are scared to death. Several physical attacks, possibly three hundred in the recent past, after he moved, displayed his ability to do great harm." My children are extremely scared of what he will do. "WE DO NOT WANT TO BE A TRAGIC NEWS-REPORT. HE NEEDS MEDICATION AND IS UNSTABLE."

I immediately went to court and filed a motion to terminate her PPO because it was all lies, fabricated to influence legal leverage in her divorce, and to gain advantage when it came to the custody hearing. I told the Judge Marlene fabricated and falsified information that is outrageous, vindictive, and evil against me. That I would never hurt my children or her, that my wife states some very wicked accusations, and she has no proof to back it up. The Judge ruled that he is going to leave it in place.

What blew me away is it's perfectly legal for any woman to walk into a court house and file a PPO ~ no investigation or questions asked! Amazing that an evil women, can walk into court, accuse the husband of abuse, file for a divorce and the systems treats her like a queen.

I was more livid at the Justice System and the Family Court Judge that would sign some order like this without doing an investigation what so ever. If that were true they should have picked me up and tossed the key away. At the very least the Court should have called family protective services. Do a major investigation or at least go visit my girls and see if they were all right.

I thought that was probably the most evil thing Marlene could have done in her life, knowing my daughters were my angels and I would never hurt them. It didn't even come close to what my beloved wife had planned out down the road.

My daughter's were my life; I loved them, protected them and did everything with them and their friends. What my wife was doing was child abuse to my daughters. Marlene told my daughters their father left them and abandoned them. On Christmas no less!

She just didn't wake up one morning and say; "I'm going to file a PPO, change the locks on the house, kick my husband to the curb and start dating Charlie today!"

The picture started to become crystal clear, very fast that this was a well thought out, and planned divorce in the workings for a long time. In court Marlene said; *"She was seeing the guy for about a year and a half."* Right about the time she started working in the bar, imagine that!

A friend of mine, told me to give my wife some time, she'll come around. I never went near Marlene or the house. I did call her often, only to plead with her to let me see my girls.

She'd always say, *"Walk away, or I'll put you away, I'm a wicked bitch!"* My girls *"will never know what I've done."* I asked if I could come over and at least get my stuff, she said; "F-you it's all mine, sucks to be you!" Speaking the most horrible, language, I've ever heard out of her mouth.

For Valentine's Day, I sent my girls two cards and my wife returned them back to me as undeliverable. I called her up and she said; "They are not your valentines anymore, they are Charlie's girls now."

I asked, Marlene if I could have Skyler for her birthday, so my family could have a party for her. Marlene said; "The girls want nothing to do with you. They like Charlie, so quit calling." My entire family was upset; we couldn't see the girls on their birthdays.

The past couple of months have been heartbreaking. I answered the phone; the female voice on the other end, told me that I need to do whatever I can to get my girls away from Marlene. The caller was very concerned about the welfare of my daughters. I never knew who it was, but they took an interest in my daughter's welfare, I thank them for that.

Today after writing this I would give anything to know who that wise woman was. I'm sure there were many more parents out there that felt the same way, along with all my daughters' school teachers. No one in my family saw Skyler for her birthday. I wasn't about to let that happen for Paris's birthday the next month, so I decided to go to the Legion and try to reason with my wife again for the sake of our children.

I went to the bar, walked in, and of course she is sitting there with Charlie again possibly getting drunk. I asked Marlene to come outside, and talk to me and she did. Charlie says; *"bring it on big boy!"* At least he wasn't brain dead and/or stupid enough to come outside, and get involved with me trying to reason with my wife, about the lives of our children.

Marlene knew that I would protect my girls at all costs. That was why she came outside with me before Charlie got too mouthy. Once outside I asked her what she was doing to our family? Marlene said; *"I don't care, about the family, just walk away!"* Then Marlene said again; *"You're never going to see the girls, I'll make sure of that. I'll put you away because the girls will never know what I've done."*

I was beyond words. I got in my car and drove off, literally beyond myself, to think about what was coming out of Marlene's mouth. That's the way Marlene talked, when she was drinking, along with taking medication prescribed by the doctor. She just didn't give a care! At this point she was past help. I was livid by the damage she was doing to our daughters, and sadly, she actually truly didn't care about our daughters or their future.

I never realized how dangerous of a woman she was, and couldn't even understand how a mother could do that to her daughters; wickedness beyond comprehension. Marlene tried every attempt possible, to have me put away in prison forever. I was about to find out why she was so adamant about wanting me out of the picture.

Little did I know, Marlene was using the court system—to advert the real truth which is about to be revealed. She was being investigated for unethical tax filings, and was trying to put the entire family debt on me using the court system to help her, before she got caught.

Until I read the passage in the Bible, "He who lives a life of sin, is of the devil." How true is that? So true it will make the hair stand up on the back of your neck. Someone e-mailed me a picture of Marlene in the bar and let me tell you in that picture she looked like the devil.

Halloween that year was interesting for her, she was wearing a bright red dress with a jet black cape, sporting a black crucifix around her neck, with her hand over her head like she's worshiping her master. Her bleached blond hair is straight and stiff, she had plastic false fangs that are hanging half out of her mouth and the darkest reddest demon eye's full of evil, which in developing the pictures can be taken out, I don't think it would have helped her.

It was so scary that you can see the devil in her. One thing for sure, if actions speak louder than words, the photo and her actions speaks volumes. She doesn't walk by the light of the day; she lives, worships and rules the darkness of night.

I became very tired of the wild goose chase Marlene had me on, not letting me or anyone in my family see our girls, for the last three months, was like torture for all of us. Not to mention she was keeping all my business paperwork, all my documents on the wage claim, my computers, laptop and clothes. It made it impossible for me to pursue the claim without my discovery documents as she had everything I owned.

I had no idea on how to pursue the wage claim from the beginning of my action, to resolve that injustice, plus I had to appear in court on my impaired driving charge. I went to court; they dropped the charges because they lost the blood sample. So they gave me my bail money back. I was glad that nightmare was finished.

I called Marlene and asked if I could get some of the furniture, which I thought was fair, we had two households of furniture and my garage was stuffed with furniture, deep freezer and a new refrigerator. Everything I needed to get an apartment until I found out what I was going to do, or where to move to. Not surprisingly Marlene said; *"F-you, I've got it all!"*

My mom told me not to worry about it. I could stay with her, until I got through divorce court. If it wasn't for the love of my mom and family, I would have been living on the streets.

"Holy Smokes", this divorce is insane. It was getting to be more than I could handle with Marlene, so I decided to see what I could do about the wage claim.

Then maybe take a vacation to Las Vegas, and try to forget about my wife, her affairs and all the things that were going on in my mind. I surely didn't need a doctor or drugs, just needed to get far away from that woman.

I've never thought about divorce, I couldn't even imagine the horrifying experiences some women go through, when their husbands leave them for another woman, after they've invested so many emotions and feelings into their marriage. Then there's the poor guy that thinks he marries a Proverbs 7 woman, then she leaves him for another man, and take's her husband's life savings.

Someone, like my wife, goes into court, admits to adultery, and the court awards the woman everything! Who came up with these laws? If you want to commit adultery and leave your spouse, do it, make up your mind and go, leave the other parent and the children out of your madness and destructive lifestyle.

I'm having all I can do to function, and try to keep my happy personality, over the whole thing and when you have kids involved it's a thousand times worse. Then you have the parent that's committing adultery, so self absorbed in their lusts they could care less about their children and what they're doing to them, because they are so blinded by sin.

Who knows what they're going to do, all I know is I needed to get away, and try to forget about the nightmare! Only place in the world, I can think of to go and try to get over my wife's affairs, is Las Vegas, Nevada.

My wife, once again, stiffed me for everything I had. I should have learned my lesson, years ago, with my Jimmy. When you have daughters, you do whatever it takes to stay with them and protect them.

With no access to any money from our joint bank accounts, the only option my wife left me was try to settle out of court with my wage claim. I'm sure her greedy, little mind was working overtime, on how she could accomplish that. About all, I can say, is *"What a woman"* and *"what the heck was I thinking when I married her!"*

Now, I know why I was having second thoughts about marrying her, back in Las Vegas before our girls were born. Maybe, I do need to go to Las Vegas, to get over her.

Chapter Thirteen

HIGH ROLLER IN VEGAS

Really ticked off over Marlene not letting me see my daughters, her adulterous affair and locking me out of our house, I called my boss who I had the wage claim against, I told him, I wanted to meet with him, and settle out of court. I called Marlene, told her that I'm going to sit down with them, present my case, and leave it in God's hands. She laughed, and hung up the phone.

No one can say what you are going to do, during a divorce. Someone in the marriage isn't going to be happy. No one can predict the outcome, or what they are going to do when the pain comes on them from the separation of their children. You have no say about your kid's welfare, because they become a statistic to the court system.

Later that week, I met with my bosses to settle my wage claim. The father and son told me they'd give me the forty four thousand dollars, they owed me for my travel expenses, and that's the best they could do. I was in no position financially to keep fighting them, so I agreed.

'What I Learned Under the Sun', is whoever has the money always wins in court, it has nothing to do with what's right or wrong, money seems to always win.

It already cost me that much over the last three years, trying to fight my claim, my boss knew that. I'm sure that my boss and his son got a good night's sleep, when I dropped the wage claim, putting their minds at ease.

I asked everyone in my family if I should give Marlene half and they said, "What are you nuts? She locked you out of your house, kept everything you own, and won't let any of us see the girls!"

"You want to give her half." Not one person felt she was entitled to any of the expense monies, because it was a reimbursement from taking her on the road traveling with me.

I told Marlene that I got an offer in the mail; all I had to do was, sign it and send it back. She was at my house in a matter of minutes, but didn't bother to bring our girls with her, so I could see them. All she wanted was a copy of the offer, so she could make a mad dash to her lawyers and try to get the money. As she's driving away yelling at me, *"That's half mine and I want it!"*

Knowing to well her plan, as she drove away, I signed it, got in my car and drove to UPS and sent it, overnight to my boss. He called the next day and said; your forty four thousand dollar expense reimbursement check is in the mail and you'll have it tomorrow.

No more did I hang up from him, Marlene called and told me not to do anything with their offer until I hear from her. I said, *"Sure honey, anything you say!"* Did she think I wouldn't see that coming? I guess her brilliant lawyer needed time to figure out how to get the money for her.

Still stressing out over her affairs, I decided to go out on the town in Montague, Michigan, where Brenda and I lived. Brenda's dad had come down to the bar, I was at, and we sat there talking for hours. I ended up going home with him, and he offered the couch for sleep.

I sat up and talked with her mom, I was so impressed with all the accomplishments Brenda did, and was never as proud of someone as much as her. That made me very happy for her and as always I loved hearing about how Rita was doing.

I woke up in the morning on the couch and started laughing to myself. I was thinking about the look Brenda would have on her face, if she walked into her mom's and found me sleeping on the couch—yea, wow!

Everyone got up and I made her mom a promise I'd get her some brook trout, hugged her goodbye, knowing our paths would cross one day again. Her dad took me out for breakfast and I headed home to get the check.

UPS came, I called Marlene and asked her if I could come over to see the girls and get my things, and she said; *"Screw you, you're not getting anything."* Then she wanted to know if I sent the offer back yet. She had no idea the check was in my possession.

Knowing very well her intentions, I went out of state to the bank where the check was drawn on, and cashed the check. Got one thousand dollars in cash to blow today, and another five thousand in cash to blow in Las Vegas, another check for six thousand dollars, one for ten thousand dollars and another for twenty two thousand dollars in case my wife let me see my daughters, I would be nice and give her half.

I went to the airport in Grand Rapids, Michigan, and booked a flight to Las Vegas. As I sat at the airport, I called Marlene and invited her to come along with me—thinking that if the money was the main issue in her head, I have it now, maybe some of the stress from the past would be gone, we could carry on a decent conversation and she said; *"I can't do that, where's my half you s.o.b.!"*

I told her have fun with Charlie and hung up the phone. If she would have let me see my girls, I would have given it all to her and she knew that!

Arguing with her at the airport, I missed my flight, so I grabbed a chauffeur. He took me to the Holiday Inn and I asked him if he would give me a ride to a Meijer's so I could buy a few things. He did, and I tipped him two hundred dollars, and he agreed to pick me up in the morning for my flight.

I didn't feel like sitting in the room so I went down to the lounge and ended up having the Hotel shuttle driver take me to a club in downtown

Grand Rapids, Michigan. I sat at the bar and played Keno and this woman cuddled up to me and literally every number I picked won.

I started getting two tickets and gave her one and she loved that. We ran the club out of money and she said; "I know another club we can go to", so she called us a cab, and off we went into the night.

At the next club the first number we played 1, 2, 3 and 4, it came out, and I couldn't keep this girl off me! She commented, take me to Las Vegas with you, I'll be your wife for the week. I promise you won't even think of your ex-wife, and I thought *"she isn't on my mind right now!"* Any other cougars (mature single woman) that came around she chased them off, I had a hard time leaving, because she almost had me convinced to take her. Then again the best way to get Marlene off my mind is to go to Las Vegas!

Rest assured anyone going through a divorce over infidelity, Las Vegas is the answer and you'll soon forget about the past. Everyone's friendly, and it has some of the most beautiful people in the world there. Interestingly enough it has some of the most colorful people also. Las Vegas is the most social place on the planet, everyone there is friendly.

I finally left and on the way back to the hotel, I'm thinking, "I've been to a club once in fifteen years of my marriage, and I go to two different clubs in one night." I felt guilty, but I know it was more so my conscience *"screaming at me"* telling me I was doing wrong by falling into a category, to the sin of lust.

The next day I got up, took a shower, went down stairs to check out, and looked outside for my driver to see if he showed up. Just as promised, the driver was waiting for me outside.

Once in the air, a million thoughts were going through my mind. More so what Marlene was doing to our family and destroying my girls.

It was after midnight before I checked into the hotel. I ordered room service and went to bed.

I woke up the next morning and had this strong urge, of being pulled to go to the chapel where we got married called; *"We've Only Just Begun Wedding Chapel."*

The force was overwhelming, so I went. I got there and they had changed the name to; *"Princess Wedding Chapel."* I stood outside; looked at the flowers, and seen the one I had for our wedding day and it almost brought tears to my eyes. The new name of the Chapel, didn't help, because I always said; "I'd get my Princess her Castle." So that made me think of my wife.

When I walked in, there was a couple sitting there, I said; *"Oh I'm sorry, I didn't think anyone was in here."* The man said; "Come on in. Are you here to get married?" I said; *"No, I got married here fifteen years ago and had this overwhelming sensation to come back."*

They both started to laugh and the woman said; "That is exactly why we're here, we got married here fifteen years ago also." Then she said; "Do you have a minute to come sit with us, we'll tell you a story about this place."

They went on and told me when they got married they both felt an overwhelming sense of peace that day as if God was at their wedding. I told them the same thing happened to my wife and me.

Long story short, they came back to seek that feeling again because of problems in their marriage. Seems the guy lost his job, his wife said, she resented him for not finding another one, distanced herself from him at home, which lead her to having an affair with a co-worker.

She said she ended up filing for a divorce, got into a bad car accident with the guy, and she almost died in the hospital.

She said when she woke up her husband was holding her hand. During the operation the Lord touched her heart, and said he was giving her one more chance. She said, as soon as she could move around, she took her husband to church and confessed her sins, and felt a thousand pounds of pressure leave her chest when she turned to the Lord.

The husband said that's why we are here, to renew our vows and thank the Lord, for giving us a second chance. They wanted to experience that feeling the day they first got married.

I told them my story was very similar. My wife was working in two bars, was having an affair and filed for a divorce. They both prayed for her, and the woman told me that you need to get back there and get your wife away from the bar, Satan has her. You need to save her, get her here to this Chapel and the Lord will do the rest.

I left and walked down the hall and forgot to ask them their names and wanted to know where they were from, so I could let them know how it went. I walked back into the chapel and they were gone. At that instant, a power came through my body like never before and I was overwhelmed with more joy than I've ever had in my life.

Looking around, I was floored because they didn't walk by me and no one was in the Chapel and I was just talking to them!

I went back to my hotel, got something to eat, and started to think about my wife again. I had no clue how to get her out of the bar and away from Satan. But my thoughts were very much different, my hatred for her disappeared, and my thoughts were more of compassion towards her.

I couldn't figure out how Charlie could be Satan, but the Bible is very clear; "If you live a life of sin ~ you are of the Devil". Committing adultery, lying with a married woman, states very clearly you get a one way ticket and it's not to paradise. It's eternal death!

I didn't even realize it, but I'd been gone for over five hours, I had no clue where the time went. I went up to the room and called my wife at the bar again. I was going to tell her about the Chapel and fly her out here. Some guy answered and said; "she's unavailable and doesn't want to talk with you" and hung up the phone.

That's cool, I thought, I went down to the bar and sat down. The waitress came over and said; *"You're sure glowing today; what can I get you?"* I'm thinking *"how can I be glowing?"* I ordered a drink and put a one hundred dollar bill in the machine, and the first hand I hit a Royal Flush came up on the deal, that absolutely blew my mind. She comes up and says; *"So you hit it Glow Boy!"* I told her, "on the first deal of all things."

As I was sitting there a young couple walked up and sat by me. She put a dollar in the slot machine, and was playing a nickel bet, and never won anything. I took a hundred dollar bill out of my pocket and put it in her machine. I told her she must have dropped it on the floor. After pleading with me it wasn't hers, I said; *"Let me show you how to do this,"* and I changed her bet from a nickel, to twenty five dollars a hand. I was hoping to win her something.

I lost the first hundred dollars, put another one in and won her eight hundred dollars, and told her to cash out! She tried to give me the money but I wouldn't let her. Then she said; "I've got to get my friends to meet you, stay here we'll be right back!"

She came back with a bunch of girls from Los Angeles, California. They were there for a beautician convention, which was pretty cool. Marlene's the one having an affair. I'm surrounded by beautiful young girls, didn't take long to get her off my mind.

I went to the rest room, and two girls each grabbed my arm and said; "We're walking with you." When I came out we were walking by a black jack table and I told them let me win you some money. They both laughed and said; "OK."

I put two hundred dollars down for all three of us, and then doubled down another two hundred dollars for each of us, the dealer busted! We all won. They were in shock; I think. Young girls in their twenties are just getting a start in life; they were broke and told me it was a blessing to them.

We went back to the bar and they invited me to go to dinner with them, I declined. Then they wanted to meet me later and I told them I'd be back here in two hours.

When they took off, another woman came up, sat by me and we started talking. I had an urge to play a hundred dollar slot machine and asked her to go with me. Off we went with our drink; I found a machine and we both sat down. I put a thousand dollars in the machine, and bet two hundred dollars, at a time. On my last pull I told her to give me a kiss for luck, if I win I'll split it with you. She kissed me, I hit the button. The machine went crazy. *We hit $25,000!!!*

She was jumping up and down hugging me, basically flipping out like some excited school girl. They came over and asked me how I wanted it. I could apply it to my account or have cash. I said; *"Cash is fine!"* They said; *"Ok, we'll be right back."*

The kiss started again, and didn't end until they came back to pay me; my adulterous wife, her affair was the farthest thing from my mind right now because I was having the time of my life in Las Vegas.

They came back with about a three stacks of bundled up one hundred dollar bills and were going to count them out. I laughed and said; *"That's not necessary, I trust you."* I gave her a stack of $10,000 and I thought she was going to faint. She said; "I can't take that from you."

I said, *"Honey! A deal is a deal and you gave me the kiss for luck, which I'll never forget!"* She said; "Are you sure?" I said, *"Yes dear, it's all yours!"*

I told her, I was running back to my room to put it in the safe and she said; "Good idea. Can I walk with you and then we'll run to my room?"

For a brief moment I laughed and thought about my wife sitting with Charlie in the Legion, kissing him for a dollar tip. If she would have come to Vegas, her first kiss, she would have gotten ten thousand dollars from her husband! Oh well; *"it sucks to be her!"*

Where was I, oh yeah, walking back to the room with a girl holding my hand and she said; "By the way, what is your name?" I said; *"Kyle."* Well Kyle, you're the nicest man I've ever met, my name is Carrie!"

We got to my room and I put the money in the wall safe and then we went to her room, which took a lot longer because she didn't know how to work the safe. I showed her real quick and then she disappeared into the bathroom. She came out looking smoking hot!

Carrie, grabbed my arm and said; "I would be honored if you let me buy you dinner tonight!" I told her that was very kind, but not necessary that I already promised some beauticians I'd meet with them.

We got in the elevator to go down and she cornered me and started kissing me wildly. She had high heels on and was my height with a sleek black dress to kill for. About the time I had my hands around her and pulled her tightly close to me, the elevator door opened onto the casino floor and we looked at each other and said; "Sh—, at the same time!"

Carrie had a drink with me at the bar. She was trying to talk me into going out with her, saying that she wanted to get to know me better and I knew without a doubt we'd end up in either her room or mine before the night was over. Not necessarily what I needed at this time. Carrie stood to leave, she grabbed both my hands, kissed me bye and told me she was going to be there for three more days and she would love to see me before she left.

I said; *"Carrie, I'll be around later tonight, maybe we'll run into each other and I hugged her goodbye!"* As she walked away from me, with more class than I've ever seen in my life in a woman; she was in her mid thirties and a gorgeous brunette, (she looked a lot like Brenda).

Her shoulder length hair was pulled back and she had a body that turned everyone's head as she walked away. Then she turned around and smiled back at me! I thought to myself, *"Are you stupid, letting her get away!"* No, just not what I needed right now.

Soon after she left, I went back into the High Roller room and put another thousand dollars in a hundred dollar slot machine, played two credits and WON again. They came back over and said; "You're on a roll, ten thousand this time!"

When she came back and paid me, she said; "In all the year's she's been there, she has never seen that happen before." The doors were opening faster than I could walk through them! What adulterous wife? Hope she's having fun, because I'm having the time of my life!!!

When I got back to the bar, the beauticians were back and we went and got a table and I bought them a round telling them about the $25,000 and $10,000 and they said; *"Cool, you can take all of us out tonight!"*

We decided to go to Pure Nightclub, one of the hottest clubs in Las Vegas. I went to the High Roller Room and had a Limo arranged to take us, my casino host called Pure Nightclub ahead of time to let them know we were coming and to reserve me the best seats in the place.

We all had another round and the six of us left and walked by a three card table. I told them to hang on, I've got a feeling girls! I sat down and put a thousand dollars on one hand and told them I'm going to win.

As they were standing around me intensely watching, the dealer deals and I reach down slowly looking at my cards. All I see is three bars and put the cards back down on the table, turn around to the girls and smiled.

I was in the last seat, so the dealer went all around the table when he got to me, he flips over my cards and I'm holding three tens and everyone at the table freaked. In one hand, I just hit thirty to one!

That was way too cool, it took them about a half hour to pay me, because they had to review the "eye in the sky" to make sure everything was on the up and up. The girls were going crazy and all of them wanted to touch me for luck. I told them we needed to go back to the bar and have a drink before we go, and then I needed to run to my room again.

We were all sitting there having the time of our lives and a guy walked up and asks; "So how is everyone doing tonight?" He was very kind, humble and obviously homeless.

I asked him to pick a number between one and ten and he looked at me puzzled, the youngest of the group just turned twenty one, leaned over me and told him; *"Dude, just pick a number!!"*

The guy looks at me and says; *"Seven!"* I told him hold out your hand and I reached in my pocket and pulled out a thousand dollar chip, laid it in his hand and told him you are absolutely correct sir, it's your *"Lucky Day!"*

He looked down and said; *"Is this real?"* and Tina, said; *"You bet, it's real!!"* I just saw him win it!" The guy freaked out, thanked me and went running through the Casino screaming to the top of his lungs. Romans 12:13, "Share with God's people who are in need, practice hospitality." I've done this all my life because it makes me feel good, helping people in need!

The only guy with us looks at me and says; *"Dude, you're that pay it forward guy, aren't you?"* I said; 'Maybe, but the one thing I do know is that I need to go cash in these chips and run to my room."

I got up and went over and tipped the waitress one hundred dollars. Tina came up and grabbed my arm and says; "I'm going with you honey!" Everyone decided to come along, I cashed the chips in, and we went to my room, I put everything but five thousand dollars in the safe. Then we all headed for the limo.

When we got to the Pure Nightclub, they escorted us to our reserved balcony. It was pretty cool, we *were* the party. I'm thinking, "It's Wednesday night, and my wife is sitting in the Legion with Charlie, and I'm sitting here with the hottest beauticians from California in Las Vegas!" Oh well; *"it sucks to be me!"*

We drank the bottle of champagne, and I ordered them another one, and told them I had to take off. I made sure everyone was alright and having a good time. Everyone hugged me, kissed me, and thanked me for a wonderful time except for one girl sitting on the sofa she gave me a kiss that took my breath away when she told me goodbye.

I almost decided to stay. She was a beautician from Los Angeles with four kids. And if things weren't so messed up at home, I would have gone with her. That's how hot the kiss was and she was gorgeous. And I love kids! Besides I was living the life of sin now, just like my wife. All I wanted was to forget her evil for not letting me see my daughters. It was working, because Marlene was the farthest thing from my mind right now!

Back at the hotel, I went to the bar to see if Carrie was around. I just couldn't get her out of my mind from the few minutes we had in the elevator. I sat there and played the video poker machine and hit it again!

So I went into the High Roller room and played video poker in there and hit it also. While I was waiting to be paid, I played the machine next to me and won the jackpot on that one too.

I walked by the bar looking for Carrie and she wasn't around, so I went to my room to put the money in my safe.

I thought about it and decided to call Marlene at the bar, (she found her way into my head again), to ask if she wanted to fly out and I'd give her all the money. Charlie answered and said, *"She doesn't want to talk to you, suck's to be you"*! Then hung up. I thought to myself *"Yep sucks to be me!"*

I called my mom. She said I had a message to call the Hesperia Village Police ~ ASAP. I did so because I was worried about my girls; something must have happened.

A month had gone by now since my last court endeavor, and to my astonishment the court issued another warrant for my arrest for that impaired driving arrest, that I thought had been dismissed. Seems someone found the blood test results that had disappeared and said they were mine.

I thought to myself, "This is a County Issue so why are the Village Hesperia Police so involved in this?" I'm thinking the whole thing stinks, especially when one Officer in particular sits in the bar everyday with my wife and she "buys" him FREE drinks.

My entire week in Vegas was like yesterday. Wherever I went, I had a beautiful woman around. No matter what I played or what casino I went to, *"I WON."* I never did run into Carrie again and was wishing I would have gotten her number.

I had so many women just randomly come up and talk with me, and that's exactly what I needed, something Marlene hasn't given me in quite some time.

No, they were not hookers, just random women on vacation with their daughters for a Hanna Montana Concert being held at the MGM Grand Hotel, my favorite place to stay when in Las Vegas.

I lost track of how many women I won money for, bought random tickets for shows or dinners for them and their daughters. Anyone who took a few moments out of their schedule to give me the time of day, to help me through the pain was a blessing to me.

Not everything had to deal with sex or be sexual; I did an act of kindness for them. Sometimes it really does pay to be nice to people!

I think, I enjoyed reaching out to mothers with their daughters, because I knew the pain my daughters were going through with their mom deceiving them, and doing everything wicked to keep them from me.

I went to Las Vegas, with five thousand dollars, and said when I lost that I'm coming home. Pretty hard to lose when everything you touch turned to Gold. I'd get down to a few hundred dollars and win another jackpot; I won jackpots all week and couldn't lose that five grand for the life of me, I couldn't even give it away and it would come back to me.

As bizarre as it seems, I ended up winning forty four jackpots for over one hundred and forty five thousand dollars, but it took one hundred and forty three thousand dollars to win those jack pots, at one hundred dollars a pull on a slot machine. I averaged three thousand two hundred and ninety five dollars a win.

I was there to have fun and forget. What a week though, and I still came home with seven thousand dollars, and tried my hardest to lose that five grand I took. I guess you have to go to Las Vegas and try your best to lose.

I had the time of my life and yes; *"Las Vegas is the best place in the world to forget about your spouse!"*

I checked out and there was a huge line for a cab. The door man told me to come with him and he took me aside from the line and hailed me a cab. A guy gets out, runs over to me and hugs me, thanking me up and down for what I did for him. It was the homeless guy I gave the thousand dollar chip to. On the way to the airport he told me I changed his life forever!

As he was getting my bags out of the trunk, he told me he was able to get an apartment with the money I had given him, buy some clothes, and had landed a job the very next day. He was hugging me goodbye as he was crying and then I started to cry. I had no idea that I could have made that much difference in someone's life from helping them out.

I thought about staying in Las Vegas, and blowing off the warrant. Then I thought about moving to California also. The reality was I had two beautiful daughters that needed their dad. I hired a lawyer over the phone while I was in Vegas to represent me. I had to meet with him in Grand Rapids, Michigan.

My flight was from Las Vegas, Nevada, to Detroit, Michigan, and then onto Grand Rapids, Michigan. When we landed in Grand Rapids, as I walked out the door, the chauffeur I hired when I left was there. He came over and grabbed my bags. I told him I have a quick stop downtown and then need a ride home and he said; "No problem sir."

When I got out of the lawyers office as we were driving home the chauffeur thanked me. Confused, I asked him; *"For what?"* He said; "The two hundred dollars you tipped me last week, was the only tip I got, and our family was out of food."

I just wanted you to know how much we appreciated it, and we prayed for a safe journey for you! Twice in one day; two total strangers have brought tears to my eyes.

When I got home, Marlene called from our house in Hesperia and said! Someone here wants to talk with you. It was the Chief of Police from Hesperia at my house! Wanting me to come there so he could take me to jail, my lawyer already advised me just to walk in the County Jail in White Cloud and turn myself in, pay a thousand dollars and they would release me. So that's what I did, no way was I going to Hesperia.

Marlene was irrate that I went to Vegas. She still wanted half the settlement. I told her you let me see my girls and I'll give you half and once again she said; *"You'll never see your girls again if you don't give me that money!"* I said; *"This is America, are you really going to hold our kids hostage?*

Then Marlene came over to the house and I still had seven thousand dollars in my pocket, I gave it to her towards child support. I figured, the house and everything in it is paid for, and I had a good idea I was going to leave for six months (after court next month), I might as well give her the money the ($7,000.00). I figured this was more than enough for the two teenage girls to get by on. I'm sure our girls never saw a penny of the money. Knowing that, I gave them each a thousand dollars to put in their bank accounts I opened for them in town.

Marlene was only worried about the money. She stormed out of the house and tore up the driveway. I don't know why she was so angry at me. I'm not the one having the affair, running around like a donkey, and making a fool of myself in the Village of Hesperia.

I called her a few days later, I wanted to share my good luck with our girls and told her I WON forty four Jackpots in Las Vegas and she said; "You're so full of it! *"That's impossible."*

I told her come on over, bring my girls and I'll show you my W2's and prove it to you! When she got here, without my girls, I showed the W2's to her and she said; *"Where's my money; I want half of that you (Expletive)"* I thought, are you kidding me? "Then Marlene grabbed my W2's and tore out the driveway. I'm sure she probably was heading straight to her lawyer."

I gave her a few weeks. I called the airlines again and made two reservations for us. I called her on a Wednesday night when I knew she was at the Legion with Charlie. I told her if she came to my house after work, I have two tickets for Las Vegas and we'll go out there and I'll give you your money. In the worse way I wanted to get her back in that Chapel in Vegas. Not all of the memories were bad or clouded and I wanted her to remember how things were. I also, knew there was a bigger reason; I had to get her back in that Chapel.

In her greedy mind she was thinking about the one hundred and forty five thousand dollars from the W2's and I was talking about half of my travel expense check I had for twenty two thousand dollars, in my brief case. But I wasn't going to let her know that.

She said; "I can't do that, I'll come over in the morning!" I told her you're not going to sleep with another man in our home and then come to see me. I don't take seconds to Satan.

She showed up in the morning with her suitcase and wanted to go. I said; too late, *"you had a choice and you made the wrong one again. I was not giving you time to clear your schedule or convince someone else you'd be back for him, you took Charlie over me again last night."* Once again she tore out of the driveway ticked off. Maybe she should *"just walk away"* from him?

Another week went by and I called her at work again, made her the same offer and got the same answer. She came over in the morning and I told her straight up it's the old man or me? And she elected to take the old man home over me so we didn't go to Las Vegas. This was the third and final time I was trying to make amends with her, I threw her three very easy balls to hit, no experience needed and the umpire yelled "Three strikes MARLENE, you're out!"

I spoke to her one more time I said; *"You have so many God given talents and you're throwing them away in the bar acting like a fool!*

It's been four months now since I've seen my girls and I told Marlene this is insane; *"I want to see my girls!"* I've been calling for them since January and every time she tells me; "The girls want nothing to do with you, if they did you would be here. They don't want to talk to you, they don't want to see you, and they can't remember you ever doing anything with them! You're a deadbeat dad and I want that money."

Since when am I not their father, why should I have to pay to see my girls? Support is one thing and visitation is another, totally separate entities.

That was really ticking me off more than anything. I'm sure she is telling my girl's their dad is a piece of crap; he walked out on you girls and wants nothing to do with you. What is sad for her; the truth always comes out in the end and I'm sure my girls aren't going to think too highly of the woman that gave them birth, when they find out what their mother really did. They were deceived and held hostage for ransom by their own mother.

Chapter Fourteen

REHAB

Forced into rehab or spending time in jail, who wouldn't pick rehab! Myself, I picked a rehab that was a "faith based Christian college." There was something drastically wrong, blood tests go missing and show up 4-5 weeks later with results so high that I must be a daily drinker to excess.

The deal my lawyer had negotiated for me at this time was a day for day credit for time served and six months sentence. I had court in a few weeks and Marlene had no idea my lawyer already made a plea deal.

My only concern was my girls. I wanted to see them before I left for six months. Marlene said; "No way; because the girls will never know what I have done!" I begged her, she said; "Screw you, you're a dead beat dad, and I will put you away, you are never going to see your girls unless you give me that money". Talk about a broken record, new song please!

But I knew I had to get my legal problem behind me, one thing at a time. Then I could start my new life whatever that would be, after college. I had to report to court on Monday before I leave for six months.

I went to court for sentencing and about died. Marlene was sitting in the parking lot. We walked into the court room, and then she walked in, sat in the back. Never once said a word to me or good luck, just sat there, with the biggest smile in the world on her face.

I was sentenced with what was agreed upon and had to go with a probation officer to another room. My lawyer said, Marlene told him, *"That's ludicrous what he got, I want him in prison."* I told my lawyer, "She was the most heartless woman I've ever known in my life."

If it wasn't for a new law our Governor signed, I wouldn't have gotten anything. I think the only one that knew about the law change, was Marlene and her cop friend. I had two OUI's fifteen years earlier when Marlene and I first met and nothing since. My lawyer told me after ten years my record would be cleared. And I thought it was.

Under the new law that just passed, law enforcement can go back on your record forever. It made a ton of money for the State of Michigan; virtually overnight from people that thought they had clean records, are now looking at Felonies with this new law. My lawyer said it hemmed a lot of people up in the State, and is generating millions for the court system.

I didn't have to go to jail because of my plea deal going to college a Christian Rehab in Detroit, I had to have them call the court when I checked in.

'*What I Learned Under the Sun*', is the day when I got home from court I had a letter from the new lawyer in Indianapolis; whom I had sent a proposal to, to handle my wage claim back in December. The firm basically guaranteed me a WIN by the end of the year on my wage claim. They had reviewed everything and would take it on contingency.

It didn't matter though, because I was forced to settle out of court. Marlene locked me out of the house, any chance I had for winning was withheld from me at the house. The evidence needed to go to the new firm for proof and she wouldn't release it to me.

For someone that was so money hungry you would have thought she would have personally taken it to the new firm. She was still involved in the outcome, we were married at that time, and contingency would have worked in her favor. I never lost Faith that I would have won the case. So it meant a lot to me knowing what the outcome would have been. Too bad she didn't have the faith. Marlene would have been pretty wealthy before the end of the year.

She probably never figured out what her affair cost her and especially our daughters. I'm not talking only financial, but what Marlene has been doing the last five months, keeping our girls from me, wasn't even close to abuse by a mother, it was mental murder!

I went from the greatest dad in the world (in my daughter's eyes), being there daily for my girls, to being the man their mother is trying to discredit just to cover up her adulterous affair and unethical handling of the family finances.

Being told by the mother that the girls don't want anything to do with you and then turning around and telling the girls their father wants nothing to do with them. The most vicious cycle of deception, I've ever experienced in my life, I can't imagine the devastation my daughters were going through.

I find it almost inconceivable that a mother would victimize her own children to cover up an adulterous affair and continue to manipulate them with false lies against their father, trying to present an image that the father is a deadbeat dad.

Then I've got people/parents calling and telling me I need to do whatever I can to get that "woman" away from your children. I knew in my heart when she said; "walk away, or I'll put you away" she was an evil woman and I was in for a long fight to save our children.

One thing that I would never do is abandon my daughters. I knew they were relying on me to find a way to save them. I know you can lose a battle and still win the war. That is what Marlene wanted, trying to alienate our daughters from me.

Marlene's plan was put in place to have me out of the picture. It was going to take a few more months before I could get in the fight to save my daughters. I had to save myself from their mother, before I could help them.

I had no idea what kind of battle lay ahead of me to save my kids or how long it would take. Rest assured I will never stop until I do save my daughters!

'What I Learned Under the Sun', is no matter what, you can never give up on your children, you have to fight for their rights, at all costs.

Chapter Fifteen

VISIONS FROM THE HOLY SPIRIT

At the Christian college, it took me a while to get use to everything, but it didn't take long to figure out the system. I had to attend church classes five times a day, and our studies were on the New Testament. We also had to attend service eight times a week. We attended a church in Novi, Michigan, by far the best church I've ever attended.

I was actually looking forward to going to a Bible college because of my premonition I had last January, when I was reading Deuteronomy 27. It was very clear to me that my purpose in life was to help people and it was all revolved around the Cross.

Up to this point in my life, every vision, basically everything I've done and everyone I've met had something to do with the Cross. At times it was overwhelming to understand, but I kept going with it even though I didn't truly understand it.

I had completed my marketing and business plan for "One Breath Away™" a tourist attraction, Christian retail store, I was thinking of opening in the future. The only thing missing was the Biblical aspects of the plan, so I was in the right place to learn.

I couldn't write anyone for thirty days, but I already had about twenty letters to send my girls and I was looking forward to that. To help pass the time I started a prayer journal for them on what I did every day.

In church everyone prayed for Marlene and our children. I had over sixty people praying for them on a daily basis including myself. On Saturday's we did a car wash for the ministry.

I was having feelings for Marlene again, letting go of the hate that was starting to build in me was like a weight off my shoulders, call me crazy but, not all the times were bad.

I hated this sinful lifestyle she lived and became very concerned for her. After spending a month in church studying about marriage, the evils of lust and adultery, I realized, I was now thinking about the time with Carrie in Las Vegas, lust could have grabbed me and took me for a ride.

One Friday night I prayed for Marlene and asked God for some kind of sign, to let me know if she is hearing our prayers? The next morning at the car wash, we had two lanes and four guys to a car. I had the front driver's quarter to wash. I took my sponge to wash the roof and window.

I turned around to do the driver's door, the suds were running down. Letters started appearing on the door, that spelled; *"Marlee!"* I about freaked out after asking God last night for a sign, if she was hearing our prayers. *"Marlee"*, is her bar nickname!

I've traveled all my life; I've never seen a name of anyone on a driver's door. What are the odds of that after asking God for a sign? Like in Las Vegas winning forty four jackpots—it was virtually impossible. Unless of course, it's comes from a Higher Power.

Then most people would look at winning forty four jackpots on slot machines in the "high limits" as sin, and nothing to do with a blessing from God. Although there is no Biblical mandate against gambling, it boils down to where your heart is, what your conscience is telling you, if it's a condemnation of the excesses.

I truly feel I was blessed to win so many jackpots because it would irritate my soon to be ex-wife to no end. That will haunt her forever and a day. Just that thought, sends her over the edge. Rightly so, she could have had it all. Then again, I was in a position to help out a lot of people at that exact moment in time, in Las Vegas.

Marlene, said, her lover, Charlie has deep pockets; he can write her a check for a few hundred grand to ease the pain he caused her. "Then again, maybe not!"

People gamble every day on the stock market and don't look at that as a sin, and it's not. It only becomes a sin when it's in excess, no matter how much you want it to be. Indeed it was impossible to win that many jackpots on "high limits" but I can assure you it happened for a reason and was all part of God's plan for His purpose, I just didn't know why!

I was very impressed with the people that graduated every month from the college. The testimonies that students gave would bring tears to your eyes, on the miracles in their lives, and how the Lord restored their families. The students here are recovering from addictions through the power of prayer; their addictions are overcome and family relationships are restored.

Thirty days flew by and I sent all the letters out to my girls. I was very excited about that and couldn't wait for them to write me back.

Another month went by and nothing, not a word. I started spending more time at night on my marketing plan. I asked God one Saturday night, if "One Breath Away™" is truly what He wants me to do, that I needed another sign.

I was going to Brightmoor Christian Church in Novi, Michigan, I prayed for a sign (ISAIAH 7:11 "Ask the LORD your God for a sign") if I'm supposed to do this, "One Breath Away™" project.

Pastor Jamie spoke that morning on 'signs'; that it's not going to be a bolt of lightning coming down, it's going to be a small circle like a silver dollar from a stranger. I thought "wow", I actually got my sign, the sermon was about signs from God.

The next morning a guy walked up to me with a shirt on that had a small circle the size of a silver dollar that said; "Charlevoix, Michigan!"

Of all the properties I looked at in Michigan, Charlevoix, was my number one choice. The guy was from Los Angeles, California, the shirt was given to him. Was this a coincidence? I think not.

You can bet I pretty much paid attention to signs after that day, because they are very real. You have to remember they are there for a reason, if you pay attention!

'What I Learned Under the Sun', is signs from God are very real, when you have eyes that can see. The only requirement is you have to ask for a sign!

Chapter Sixteen

WICKEDNESS BEYOND COMPREHENSION

Summer was here, the ministry was having their annual 4th of July, Family picnic. The ministry sent invitations to everyone's families. I was the only one that didn't receive back a confirmation that was sent out to their families. Imagine that, Marlene is still holding my girls hostage.

I still haven't received any letters from my girls, so I sent them another one telling them how much fun it would be on the 4th of July, if they could come to the family picnic. I wanted them to meet all my new friends here. In the letter, I told them Grandma would be happy to bring them if their mother would let them come.

The day came and everyone's families showed up. I sat in the church window praying for mine, that I would see them drive in. I never gave up, I prayed the entire time. Then everyone started to leave, and I realized I would not be seeing my girls today. I didn't give up hope.

Marlene held the power of good and evil within her, apparently she chose not to allow my daughters come visit their father.

On July 21st, my life was changed forever. I received a Judgment of Divorce in the mail. Marlene's lawyer entered a Quickie Divorce Judgment two weeks before our actual hearing was scheduled in court. It was the worst horrifying document I've ever read in my entire life.

Marlene couldn't have done anything more wickedly to her family than what she was doing to our girls. Just to cover up her adulterous affair she was willing to destroy her own daughters with deception and lies to cover her own addictions and selfishness.

When I read what she had in the divorce papers, I had so much hatred for her it was beyond words, the pain of what she was doing to my daughters was unbearable, if not child abuse by a mother, more like the worse kind of mental abuse imaginable.

I tossed the Judgment of Divorce on my desk, and was just beside myself, at that instant the Holy Spirit came on me and changed my life forever.

When the Holy Spirit came the pain instantly went away, I was overwhelmed with Joy, Love, Peace, and Happiness. I had no more hatred towards Marlene, but felt deep love for her. Something I never felt in my life. I never felt so weird.

There was no hatred, no hurt, no bitterness, no pain, and no exhaustion. All those feelings take so much energy just to have them, once resolved, a newly energized lease-on-life emerges.

Maybe I had it all along and just didn't realize it, but other people seemed to see the light in me. But it was real, it was powerful, and it was overwhelming! It's very weird; few adults see it, but from my experience young kids sense it instantly.

It's hard to explain when the Holy Spirit comes on you exactly what happens. Darkness leaves your body, and you're filled with an overwhelming sensation of joy that comes only from the heart. That's the secret; it comes from the heart.

Looking back, that was the same thing that happened to me in the Chapel with that couple, when they told me to get my wife away from Satan. I can only imagine what would have happened if I could have gotten Marlene away from Charlie and back to the Chapel where we were married!

Looking back now I probably should have swallowed my pride, and took her when she showed up in the morning! But being a dominate lion; I wasn't taking seconds to no one.

Only if I would have known about true justice; showing my wife compassion, mercy, forgiveness, and grace that can only come from the power of the Holy Spirit! I do know that she was not ready to accept what I had to offer her for the sake of our family.

I often thought about that couple and my only conclusion comes from my favorite scripture: Hebrews 13:2 *"Do not forget to entertain strangers, for by so doing some people have entertained angels without knowing it."*

Just by the way they mysteriously disappeared, what they talked about, and the blessings "luck" that followed me after our paths crossed, angels are now a good description for them.

My thoughts then drifted back to Brenda that day at the airport waiting for me, did she encounter an Angel to comfort her. Angel's are very real; *"we make them laugh"* most of the time.

I was so over-powered with joy, I was in tears. Walking to class everyone is like; "what's so funny?" I sat in the front row in church; I couldn't stop laughing, no matter what.

Afterwards the pastor said; "Kyle, I see you're filled with the Spirit today!" The Spirit never left me, even a week later I was asked to step out of class because I was overwhelmed with so much joy, I couldn't control it.

'What I Learned Under the Sun', is that the Spirit is "Sensitive" to your thoughts and actions. When you realize your body is a temple of the Holy Spirit, who lives in you, whom you have received from God, your thoughts and ways change forever. The key is your heart!

You have to be of the light, and you have to turn from darkness to receive it. I can tell you one thing that pride is a killer; you have to *humble* yourself, which comes from within your heart.

I've always had faith, but never really read the Bible because I was reading a King James Version and it was just too difficult for me to understand. When I arrived here, I was given a NIV Bible (New International Version).

I became so intrigued with the stories in the Bible; I read its entirety multiple times and even highlighted scriptures that had the most meaning in my life.

The Holy Spirit is very real. The Bible is very powerful; it will change your life forever, if you turn from darkness. A lot of people have hope, but they miss one thing in their life; faith!

To get it, you have to turn from darkness, come into the light and God will do the rest, in an instant, any addiction can be cured, I saw living proof of that every day in church.

Another time, we were going to church on the bus. I was sitting in the middle by the window and we were on a two-lane highway. There was a car next to the bus and I was looking out the window. A little girl about eight years old in the back seat bends forward turns and looks me straight in the eyes and gave me the biggest smile I've ever seen in my life, and then we drove off.

I thought that was a little strange, until it happened again when we were driving down the road. Someone is sitting by every window on the bus, this car is driving beside us on the same two-lane highway, and this very attractive blonde was staring at me, never took her eyes off me going down the road. As her car started to pass the bus she even turned around staring at me until she was out of sight.

We never smiled at each other, but never took our eyes off each other, and everyone on the bus wanted to know why she was staring at me! I don't know to this day what she saw or felt in my presence, but there was definitely something going on that they were drawn to me!

One thing I enjoyed while there, any new guys that came in I would always buy them something from the store so they felt welcomed. Lots of people came through the doors with just the shirt on their backs and needed a friend to build them up at the lowest point in their lives. They needed someone to help build them up; not tear them down.

I was a cook in the kitchen, I made all the salads, not once did I make a salad the same. I always made them special, so everyone had something to look forward to everyday. On the 4th of July, I made a salad with fireworks out of fruit and cheese. Another time I made one look like the State of Michigan with the Mackinac Bridge.

The women's supervisor told me I was a very colorful guy! Whatever you're dealt in life, you exceed at it, make it enjoyable; taking it to the next level and I believe that with any job I do, even if I'm not getting paid to do it.

Fall was here and we were having a Labor Day party for everyone's families again, and as before, the ministry sent out the invitations to everyone's families. I've been here almost six months and still never received one letter from my girls; I have a feeling they were writing me but the letters just weren't being sent. I'm sure of that.

Isn't my wife a blessing, to her husband and daughters! Ya' gotta Love Her!

My angels wouldn't forget their dad, and I knew they loved me with all their heart and soul. My girls are the world to me and Marlene knew that. I spent my life protecting them and making sure they were taken care of. I didn't even allow my girls to walk a block to school, I thought it was my duty as a Father to drive them and make sure they made it safely.

A parent's life is a child's guidebook. Marlene had become so overwhelmed with evil that she actually thought she was doing no wrong; that it's a new age of sex, drugs, and rock and roll.

I learned the saddest part of blindness to her affair, was what she was teaching our girls; living an adulterous life with Charlie wasn't wrong, it's alright to get a divorce and live a life of sin.

I was fortunate enough to talk with Paris on the phone one time in six months; she was so excited her mother broke up with Charlie. No child wants their parents divorced, in her heart; I knew what she wanted, but for the fear of her mother she couldn't ever talk about it.

The entire time Marlene was deceiving my girls, telling them their dad left them and wants nothing to do with them. Then every time I called to see the girls she would tell me they want nothing to do with me. It became a vicious-cycle of deception that Marlene played over and over.

Marlene was in the bar seven nights a week and bringing parties home to my girls. It didn't take long for her lack of discipline to catch up with our daughters. My angel, Paris went from an A student to failing, all within a year under the guidance of her mother. She was kicked out of school five times, in six months and Marlene said her lifestyle had no effects on our daughters.

'What I Learned Under the Sun', is that when you turn from God to sin, and worship the devil, you become the devil's advocate, and then destruction follows. Marlene absolutely sees no wrong in it, but in reality she is actually murdering her own children's innocence, over her selfishness of addictions, adultery, and lusts.

What bothered me the most was that my angels went from having a dad that took care of them, with discipline in their lives, to being left alone at home without supervision!

Marlene turned our daughter's world upside down for the life of sin. I felt in my heart, it's her affair, she should have done what was right, just leave the marriage, and ride off into the sunset with Charlie. She should have left our daughters out of her mess.

It's like if you want to go commit adultery, it's your life, go do it, but don't drag your innocent children into your lifestyle. Just because you don't have any respect for yourself; don't disrespect your husband and put your children through hell, because you're blinded by sin.

I'm very blessed that God opened my eyes with Marlene. I still have time to find a loving wife that I can grow old with, respect, and have a blessed life.

I couldn't even comprehend being married to someone I didn't even know, who was so deceptive, it just blows my mind I just wasted so many years living a life of deception, and there was never any love in the marriage.

'What I Learned Under the Sun', is scripture is very real, the difference between a Proverbs 7 woman (Warning against the Adulteress), and the Proverbs 31 woman (Sayings of King Lemuel, "A wife of noble character who can find? She is worth far more than rubies."), is exactly as the Bible says it and its there for a reason!

I never understood how I was so deceived by Marlene; she showed her true colors during the divorce. She always denied the affair with Charlie, but during the entire divorce, she paraded him in court like her puppet. I couldn't imagine anyone with respect or class going into divorce court with your lover, and flaunting it in the face of your soul mate and God.

Marlene actually thought sitting on his lap in court was going to bother me. How old is she anyway? Old enough to know better, talk about disrespect. Wow; every time I saw Charlie walk in court with her, I thanked God that he saved me from such an evil woman.

Flaunting some old man (senior citizen) in court to make me jealous really didn't have much effect on me. Any woman can go to any bar and find a drunk.

About the only thing in the world, I could think of, that I would want from my soon to be ex-wife is her wedding dress.

I think it would be awesome to have a big bonfire, have all my friends over and watch that white dress go up in smoke!

I personally couldn't think of a better way to have closure with my marriage to Marlene than burn her wedding dress. It would be like sending her marriage vows up in smoke to heaven!

Now I'm feeling the Love!

I'm a very sentimental man, always have been. Marlene kept all my daughters' photographs, and wouldn't allow me to have any. Why? She knew that would afflict the most pain on me, trying to wipe my girls out of my life, not having any memories of them or us together.

If, I could have anything from my marriage it would be one thing. All my daughters' photos and videos, I'll get them one day! Just like, my daughters and I will make new memories that will last a lifetime with my angels.

I struggled every day, trying not to have ill feelings towards the woman that took my kids hostage and destroyed their lives.

I find it even harder to pray for her and bless her life, but even through all her evil I still try to show her love and compassion, by praying for her.

If you want to walk in the Light, you have to guard your mind against lust, and develop love. The fight for Jesus is the most important fight you'll have in your life. He is the only way to true happiness.

'What I Learned Under the Sun', is the hardest lesson in life is making the right choices. Regardless of how you try to present yourself or justify your sins, the truth will always come out in the end!

Like my boss and his son, that cheated me out of my commissions. In his mind; his "name" made him a millionaire that resulted in significant sales growth and with the sales of his company, he donated a few bucks to the Catholic Services and he's got his ticket to heaven.

That's not, how God works; God brought the right people into his life at the right time to double his sales for three years; which resulted in significant growth, that the investor looked at. *'What I Learned Under the Sun'*, is Gods timing is perfect, He brought all the right people in place for my boss's success.

That is where God gives us free will to do what's right.

That is what determines your future.

'What I Learned Under the Sun', is your actions come from within your heart, you have to guard your heart at all costs, that's reality. Jesus is the only way to heaven, and that's the ticket to heaven!

'What I Learned Under the Sun', is if you walk by faith, love always perseveres, love never fails. Trust in God even in the most difficult circumstances in your life, He will open up all the right doors for you. God uses pain and difficulties to draw us closer to Him, so we make changes in our lives. He never gives you any more than what we can handle. Trials are tests, to help us to grow spiritually. The Holy Spirit will come into your life when you love God with all your heart, mind and soul.

'What I Learned Under the Sun', is you have to change your thoughts and that will determine your future. If you want to change your behavior you have to change the way you think!

To develop love you have to have the love of Christ. Great love leads to great hatred when wronged, forgiveness leads to reconciliation. Kind words will always save a strained relationship; you need to tame the tongue, "love covers over all wrongs."

'What I Learned Under the Sun', is holding onto bitterness, is like a poison and it will eat you alive.

'What I Learned Under the Sun', is that holding onto that bitterness of poison, will take you down to the depths of hell; it shapes the outlook on your life, the kind of relationship you have, and how you treat your family and loved ones.

You become stuck; the only thing you think about is yourself and your addictions.

'What I Learned Under the Sun', is that the evil of bitterness will leave you in a dark state of being; you have no self-worth and it's emotionally paralyzing. If you live in darkness, it physically drains you and spiritually hardens your heart so you can't heal.

The moment you tell yourself, "God I've had enough; I can't take it anymore." In an instant He will restore your faith, turn darkness into light, take all your pain away, and overwhelm you with joy.

God desires that we walk in His ways, but He does not force His ways upon us. Don't try to blame God or Satan for your choices; it's your responsibility, it's called; *"Free Will"*, you have a choice on what door you walk through.

'What I Learned Under the Sun', is that your spiritual position and your eternal destiny are the only two things you know with certainty and no amount of money in the world can buy it.

'What I Learned Under the Sun', is there isn't a drug, drink, or high that can compare to the Holy Spirit in you.

It's a high you can't explain, it comes from the heart and it's magnificent beyond comprehension only if you've been filled with the Spirit do you know the overwhelming joy it brings.

When it happens, nothing can compare to that feeling when you're in the light. Everything does happen for a reason under the sun and my time is almost up here in court ordered rehab, and I get to move on with my life, doing everything in my power to get my girls back.

Chapter Seventeen

IMPRISONED

Saturday night was here again, I had less than a few weeks to go and my six months would be up, and I asked God for another sign. During services next morning a new guy was acting out and I thought silently to myself he isn't going to be good for anyone.

I walked out of church disappointed. I didn't get a sign. On the church bus that same guy sat in front of me. As we're going down the road he turns around to me and says; *"You build it, they will come."* Almost the exact same words I heard in a movie not too long ago. I asked him why he said that to me and he said; "I don't know." Well, that pretty much blew me away!

So I had no hesitation that when I left Bible college (rehab) I was supposed to do what God planned for me all along; to help kids and build; *"One Breath Away™"*, that was going to be a big part of my future one day.

What I thought was even more amazing, I have judged someone innocently for no reason other than the way they acted in church, and ironically the person I judged, God used to give me a message. That's how God works.

It's hard to recognize signs but when you get the hang of it, they become crystal clear and they are always there; you just have to open your eyes to see them.

Finally; I got mail today, but it wasn't the kind of mail I was looking for! It was from a cop that had a warrant for my arrest from the Friend of the Court. Marlene was hauling me into court for a support hearing two weeks before I completed my court ordered rehab.

I've **NEVER** had my day in court over the divorce. My wife's lawyer did a seven day quickie divorce, by law I was entitled to a property and custody hearing. Because of the lies, she put in the PPO, the court looked at me like I was piece of trash. The court system judged me, and convicted me before I even had a hearing, based on my wife's deception.

I was required to report to probation when I left rehab. I received the warrant, went straight to the probation office, and reported as required, before the court hearing.

I showed my probation officer the paperwork, which stated I was required to be in court on a felony support hearing. As I was sitting at his desk, he got a phone call and I heard him say; that's very interesting because he is sitting in front of me right now!

The probation officer said it was a female caller on the other end of the line that told him, that I left rehab and wasn't welcomed back. Then he said; "Damn if you do, damn if you don't, but I'm going to arrest you anyway for leaving rehab on a court order." He had me arrested and jailed without even having a probation violation hearing.

I'm amazed that our legal system can allow someone as a probation officer that much power to make a decision, taking six months of your life away from you and your children. You wonder how many more lives that man destroyed, abusing his power of authority and violating people's civil rights.

I had two weeks left on my six month sentence and now I had to do my six months all over again in jail, because my probation officer violated my civil rights and didn't even allow me a probation violation hearings.

'What I Learned Under the Sun', is if someone in authority wants to put you in jail, they can put you there, and there isn't a thing you can do about it until you are released. Make no mistake about it, I wasn't even allowed to hire a lawyer or even have a hearing.

And "I saw something else under the sun:" In the place of judgment—wickedness was there, in the place of justice—wickedness was there. Ecclesiastes 3:16

You think a guy would be enraged? But it didn't bother me a bit, it wasn't my time and I know now everything happens for a reason in life. I was on God's time and if He wanted me here that's where I'm supposed to be.

Maybe someone needed protection, help, or saved, but the Lord had me here for a reason. I quit trying to understand it in college.

'What I Learned Under the Sun', is everything happens for a reason under the sun, it's the will of God why things happen, you just have to have faith in God's plan.

Sometimes people just don't understand that because God has a better plan for us, more than we could ever imagine, all you have to do is have faith against seemingly insurmountable odds.

After they booked me in jail, the CO (Corrections Officer) made me an outside trustee, put me in the trustee suite downstairs, with private restrooms, showers, and its own living room.

A few days later they shackled me, hauled me into court for the FOC (Friend of the Court) charge for Felony Support, when I've never even had a custody hearing yet.

When I walked through the hallway to court, Marlene and her son were sitting there in the hallway, laughing hysterically at me. (Six months later when I got out of jail I had subpoenaed the phone records from college, to see if anyone from there made a call to my probation officer's area code).

Detroit, Michigan, was a different area code, than White Cloud, Michigan. Not one phone number was recorded being made to area code 231, so who ever made that call to my probation officer wasn't who they said they were.

I saw more evil in Marlene at that moment then I've ever seen in my life. I thought to myself, "how pathetic of a person she had become to the life of sin, and has no fear of the Lord."

If she thought I looked like "Cool Hand Luke" in Alabama, when she saw me, I wonder who she thought I looked like this time, when she saw me walk into court, because I looked like one "Bad Boy" or like her boyfriend says; "Big Boy". I'd been working out for six months straight in the weight room at college. I was probably in the best shape of my life, and that's a good thing when you get innocently tossed into Jail.

I saw another mother from school in the hallway and I'm sure she thought the same thing when she looked at me. I asked God for strength, I'm telling you he gave me physical strength, my body was rock solid and my arms we're huge from working out in the weight room for six months.

My wife was sitting there laughing, and I truly felt compassion and sorrow for her because of; Proverbs 11:8 *"The righteous man is rescued from trouble, and it comes on the wicked instead."* I fear for her because the Lord will take revenge on my behalf in this lifetime for her wickedness against me and my daughters you can be sure of that.

'*What I Learned Under the Sun*', is a man reaps what he sows. Our actions, good or bad, have consequences. We "*reap*" the consequences of the deeds we have done.

No matter how you try to paint a rosy picture, justify your actions that it's alright to live an adulterous life. The Bible is very clear about adultery, make no mistake about it; to lay with a married woman is eternal death no matter how hard you try to justify it in your human mind.

I take no pleasure in the death of the wicked, one can only hope and pray that they turn from their ways and live.

They parade me into the court room on the FOC charge. The first thing, Marlene tells the Referee; *"Your Honor, he was out partying all night and came home, and caused all kinds of problems for me and my girls!"* I was like blown away in court with the lies coming out of her mouth. I asked the Referee, to let me hire a lawyer. He said; I couldn't, that he would appoint one for me and then set another court date for the felony support hearing.

The day comes and back into court I go. Can you imagine the Referee, appointed me a lawyer from Hesperia, and the first words out of his mouth to me was; *"You're a piece of crap, pay the woman, you're getting 90 day's!"* I still have never had a hearing on child custody or the divorce. The court gave me another 90 days for felony support to be served concurrent for child support I didn't even owe.

No investigation, nothing, your just guilty as charged and you're supposed to shut up, and do your time. I wasn't surprised; about what she said in court. This was the first time I laid eyes on her in eight months and under oath she still has no fear of the Lord, and lies in court.

They should have tossed her in prison right on the spot for committing perjury. I was in court on a felony support warrant for child support, not drunk driving like she told the court. I was beyond words to what I was witnessing. An entire court system was looking at me like a piece of trash while she was running around dancing on the bars, celebrating, and trying to get me in prison on felony support charges.

Then I was sentenced another three months, I still hadn't had my day in court for custody or the divorce. The FOC used fraudulent numbers, inflated my child support, accumulated support retroactive to the time I was in rehab and unavailable to work, so they could issue a show cause and get me locked up in jail.

Still no custody hearing, and I've never met anyone from the FOC regarding child support, they didn't even apply that seven thousand dollars, I gave my wife towards support.

I was locked up most of the year, unavailable to work and made just a little over three thousand dollars for the year. Yet the FOC calculated my support at two thousand two hundred dollars a month, based on what my wife told them my income was. By law they are required to acknowledge my Federal 1040 and the courts wouldn't even look at it as evidence.

So they hauled me back to jail AGAIN. I still haven't seen my daughters and they're only twenty minutes away from the jailhouse. I wouldn't see day light until next year. I'm just beyond myself that this can even happen in the legal system and there is nothing I can do about it until I get out of jail.

In jail there is no sense of time, you're just there marking the days off your calendar. Some days went so slow that I would mark two or three weeks off at a time to speed up time.

When you're doing time, you can make it pleasant or miserable, it's like "free will" and it's your choice. I made the choice to make it as pleasant for everyone that came across my path as I could.

Everyone pretty much liked me in jail. I never got any visitors but one Saturday my name was down, they never called me for the visit, because who ever called to visit me changed their mind. I would have given anything to know who it was.

A friend named Rodney wanted to set me up with his aunt so I would have a visitor. He wrote her a letter and a few weeks went by. That's all everyone talked in jail about was getting a "dove" for Kyle.

A few months later on Saturday, my name is down that I have a visitor, I go up at my time and sit in a booth and no one comes in.

The CO tells me, "Don't you even know your own people? Right down there is your visit." I turned and looked, and said; *"That little old lady is my visit?"*

I walked out of my booth, went down to the end booth where she was sitting and picked up the phone. She has this hooded sweatshirt pulled up over her head barely peaking out. Then this little old lady says; *"Hello!"* I said; *"Wow ~ you're my visit?"*

I talked to her for a short time, told her she had the wrong guy. That a guy named; Kelly wanted to visit her and told her to have a great day! Kelly was my partner outside, the nicest guy you'd ever want to meet in the world. He also got into trouble with that new law change just as I did.

When I got back to my suite (cell) and told the story, everyone was in tears laughing. No matter where I'm at, in sin city or jail spiritual things were constantly happening to me. Now more than ever since the Holy Spirit came on me and I have eyes that can see again.

Be it an inmate or corrections officer, the ones that were evil had fear of me and they knew I could sense the evil within them. There was no doubt about that!

They stayed far from me because they feared the power of the Lord. One guard that was a sergeant finally couldn't take it any longer and put the power of the Lord to the test. He took my Bible and cursed me. When the officer grabbed my Bible out of my hand, he almost went into convulsions and started to lose it, shaking and cursing uncontrollably like some madman.

I told everyone in the suite about what happened, I told them that, the man will be broke down within days. It was exactly two days, my Bible was returned to me and the sergeant was broke down to the lowest rank possible and given the worst job duty in jail working c-floor. Then he had to work with another friend of mine a trustee called; "Billy Jack" so that was going to be a treat, because he liked Billy Jack, as well as he liked me.

There was another guy in the suite that would sit up all night, and just stare at me with his jet black shark eyes. Word got out that he made a shank out of a razor blade, and was going to slit my throat at night when I slept.

They broke him down, and moved him out. I wish they would have left him in there to try. He wouldn't have gotten very close to me, and would have seen firsthand the wrath of the power of the Lord. 1Samuel 2:9 *"He will guard the feet of his saints, but the wicked will be silenced in darkness."* I had no fear of anyone in jail.

Once we had a new tough guy come into the suite, I was reading the Bible on my bunk, and someone told him to kick my butt! He looked at me and said; *"Are you nuts, he has the power of the Lord!"* At the moment I was reading; Joshua 23:9-10 *"One of you routs a thousand, because the Lord your God fights for you, just as he promised. So be very careful to love the Lord your God."*

The signs have been never ending, above the door was a picture of Jesus, I took it down and read it. It was a post card and on the back it was from my only competitor for "One Breath Away™" in North Carolina, once again, what are the odds of that?

Kelly and I spent from six in the morning to seven at night in the garage outside. We had our own coffee pot and TV. Cops brought us food and sodas all the time. Life was tough doing hard time.

We did have to clean the Sheriff's Department and one of the female officer's there constantly came around, I just blew her off all the time. One time she tried to corner me in the supply closet, I slipped by her and took off out the door. She followed me outside and told me to come back, and bring Kelly with you!

I told Kelly about it, and said; *"come on we've got to go back!"* We walked into the kitchen; she started to yell at Kelly that I'm not giving her enough attention! Kelly said, what the heck do you want me to do about it?

Then her husband walked in, we both left and when we got outside, I started laughing and Kelly said; "Yea-Wow!" It seemed like a day didn't go by without some kind of excitement going on.

The six months I was there, over, seventy prisoners came through my suite. This one new guy was talking about doing Bible studies. I told him I'd be interested in something like that and he said; "he has one left!"

I said; *"Don't tell me it's Deuteronomy?"* He said; "how the heck did you know that!" That's the only thing it could have been with all the signs from God, his vision from Deuteronomy 27 to me, what else, could it have been!

Every time a new prisoner came in, I would buy them a commissary bag so they had everything they needed to make their stay more comfortable. I could not sit there, watch someone doing time because they were poor, couldn't pay a fine, and had to go to jail to work off their fines. Then for them to have to, watch everyone eat, when they didn't have money to buy a bag of commissary. I always made sure everyone was taken care of.

Some inmates, I call them the young ones, Kids in their teens would hang on me like glue. Most of them wanted me to be their dad and called me dad. They all had something in common; they came from broken homes.

Their parents were divorced and they had no father figure in their lives. It really opens your eyes to the damage divorce causes, how much help our youth in this generation needs.

I'm almost positive that's why I was in there to learn that because my vision for "One Breath Away™" was all about helping people in need,

I'm not sure if helping prisoners would have been in my future game plan. I'm pretty positive it wouldn't have been. Now it's going to be a very big part of my campaign in helping people.

I was amazed the amount of poor people in jail only because they were poor and couldn't afford to pay a traffic fine. They get a citation/ticket, and the court fines them. They don't pay it, are brought back into court; the Judge triples the fine and gives them so many days to pay it. Then if it's not paid, they are brought back into court on a contempt charge and ordered to jail on the spot. It's called; "Pay or stay." They can get out of jail, if they find someone to pay their fine, or they stay in jail and get ten dollars a day credit towards the fine. When they accumulate enough days to cover the fine, they can be released from the system.

It truly blew my mind. I thought debtors' prisons were abolished in the United States in the 19th century. I did a little research and found out whether a debtor is locked up depends largely on where the person lives, because enforcement is inconsistent from state to state, and even county to county. Trust me, it happens.

I'm seeing some very scary trends, especially when the court system starts violating your civil rights and I'm sure that's also from county to county, depending on where you live.

'What I Learned Under the Sun', is you better do everything in your 'POWER' to keep your children out of the court system, that is probably the most important advice I could give any loving parent. Families better start coming together, becoming self-sufficient and stop relying on the system.

One day a young kid came up to Kelly and me, and said; "Go into the bathroom, he had this awful look on his face and you knew it was bad!" We went into the bathroom, there was a sheet over the shower for a door, and it was soaked in blood. Kelly pulled the sheet back; a seventeen year old had tried to commit suicide by slitting both his wrists. I prayed for him and he lived to see another day.

The guards came and took him out on a stretcher to the hospital. He was back within three hours in the holding tank. I was shocked! The kid should not have been in jail. He needed psychiatric help. People have no compassion, nor do they show mercy to people in need. Sometimes you have to open your eyes and ask yourself; "What would Jesus do!"

It was starting to get cold outside so I told my "Host" the New Sergeant that I wanted to work in the kitchen. Kelly was leaving and I didn't want to spend the winter outside.

I asked God to put me there and I prayed for him to bring a girlfriend in my life. I needed a female companion in my life because I was starting to get restless, and no one in my cell wanted to see me to get restless!

December was here and there was another inmate, named Wayne that was to be released on the 30th. He had two wonderful daughters. I wrote his Judge, and asked him, if Wayne could be released a week early. I would do the remainder of his time for him so he could be with his girls on Christmas morning.

The judge wrote back that he would have to get a lawyer, set a court date for a hearing, by the time the poor guy did all that, he would have been out anyway. But I tried, helping him out so he could spend Christmas morning with his daughters.

Loving the Holiday's like I do, no matter what, trying to spread the Holiday gift of giving the best way I could. I would do additional jail time for any father, so he could spend Christmas with his children. Since my wife was keeping mine from me, being only twenty minutes away.

I had another inmate who took a liking to me, named Mark, he was in a bunk across from me. When he left he gave me a book, signed the inside cover saying; "Kyle; God has a reason for everything, I believe

I was destined to kick it with you here. Don't be a stranger see you in future chapters, your pal Mark."

Mark had no idea but I knew him when his band played in Montague, Michigan years before when I was with Brenda, let's say we both knew him and keep it at that. Sure is a small world we live in.

The day after Kelly was released, my Host put me in the kitchen and I became the kool-aid guy! My new boss was a very attractive brunette named Sherry and by the time I left we became very good friends. Like they say careful what you pray for, you just might get it!

Sherry made my days very pleasant and I looked forward to seeing her every day. It was like she was a true blessing to me, because she had already gone through, what I now was going through with my daughters.

My time was flying by in the kitchen, Christmas was a few weeks away and I was looking forward to the New Year because my plan when I got released was to save my girls, no matter what the cost.

Chapter Eighteen

MORNING STAR RISES IN YOUR HEART

They say you have one true friend in your life closer than a brother, if you're incarcerated, you find out real quick who your friends are. When the visitation list was posted again, I was shocked that I had a second visitor, I was praying it was my girls and not, *"that little old lady."*

I can't even express the feeling of having a visitor after so long, the intensity of not knowing who it is was overwhelming, because you don't even know what visitor booth to go in to.

I walked by the visitor's windows looking, here sits a *"Hot Blonde"* with her back to the window, I was the happiest guy in the world, when I saw who it was. It was a long-time friend from school, and her name was Morning Star.

She gave me a big smile, asked me how I was doing. I said; *"Great as can be!"*

Then she asked; "Have you had a lot of people come visit?"

I said; *"Nope, you're the first in nine months!"*

She got tears in her eyes and said; *"Kyle, that's the saddest thing, I've ever heard."* You're kids haven't even come to see you? I said; no the ex-wife is still holding them hostage.

We only had an hour to visit and the time flew by. When she left, I had tears in my eyes. I was so happy to see her and I think she felt the same when she left.

That night I thanked God for answering my prayers. That's the power of the Lord. He brought not one but two women into my life in one week, and got me back in the kitchen from the cold outside.

Then I said another prayer that I hope Morning Star was single and that I'm in her heart. I opened up my Bible to read and turned to; 2 Peter 1:19 and read; *"the morning star rises in your heart."* I literally froze in time and was instantly overwhelmed again with the Spirit of Joy.

She told me, she would write me, about three days later, I got my first letter in the mail in a year, outside of my immediate family. A fourteen page letter from Morning Star, I was bursting with joy. I don't know if she'll ever know how much that letter meant to me right before Christmas being my favorite time of the year.

We started writing each other every day, and she came to visit me on Saturdays. That gave me something to look forward to, what a blessing. Everyone in jail nicknamed her my "Dove".

When I left college there was a dove around me all the time. When I got to jail and became an outside trustee, my first days outside there were two doves across the street in a tree. They were there every day. Finally, Kelly, would just say; *"Kyle, here's your doves!"*

I don't take anything for granted when it comes to signs or strange things, because they are there for a reason if you pay attention. A dove is sensitive to the Holy Spirit, and represents Love, overwhelming love.

Why do I have two doves always around me? I believe the two doves are a sign to me that the Lord is protecting my two daughters; Paris and Skyler, keeping them safe while my ex-wife has me locked up in jail.

Christmas was almost here so I ordered twenty, 100 Grand Candy Bars for all the guards. I was going to wrap them in sandwich bags with a special scripture I picked out of the Bible for each guard that best fit their personalities.

One of the inmates made a bet with another inmate. He was sitting all depressed on his bunk because, he couldn't pay up. I pulled my tray out from under my bunk, grabbed the candy bars, walked over to him and said; *"Pay your debt and don't bet again!"*

I had to take care of this kid all the time in there. Tough luck for the guards; I'm glad they didn't know or they would have probably put me in the tank for giving their candy bars away.

I got a letter from Morning Star the day before Christmas and I waited until Christmas Eve to open it. She sent me a bunch of pictures of her and put perfume in the letter.

That was the most special Christmas. It meant more to me than anything in the world considering I wasn't with my daughters. My wife was still holding my daughters hostage. Only twenty minutes away, I knew Marlene wasn't going to bring my daughters to see me on Christmas, that's the kind of woman she is!

I taped Morning Star's picture on top of my bunk, before I went to sleep I thanked God for bringing her into my life. One night I was holding my Bible in my hand; one of her pictures fell down and landed on the Bible.

It was a glamour shot of her with a burgundy background. It landed perfectly in the center of my Bible on the back cover and stuck there. What are the odds; her background in the photo matched perfectly to my Bible, imagine that!

I was falling in love with Morning Star from her letters, we both wanted to see where it would go when I got out. She told me I wrote the most beautiful letters to her, but it was her that wrote the most beautiful letters to me.

I wrote her daily. On New Years, I told her she was in my heart. I got her letter and basically she said the same thing. That she sat home thinking of me.

Some days I would get two letters from her and she would get three from me. It was amazing how much we had in common with each other. I just knew when our lips met "Heaven and Earth would Collide!"

Sherry had to work New Years Day, so that made my day all the more special. I enjoyed being around her and missed her when she wasn't working. She told me the first day she seen me outside; *"I was glowing!"* Instantly goose bumps came over me. This is the third woman within a year that has told me I was glowing. It was sort of starting to freak me out because every time I heard those words big things happened in my life.

Sherry was married, but we did have a special bond together. We definitely had the chemistry together for a great friendship. I knew God brought her there to get me through doing hard time; there was no doubt about that.

With the New Years here, having only five weeks to go before my out date, I had no idea how I was going to make it. I just wanted to be with Morning Star, she wrote me such beautiful letters. Time almost stopped when I read them.

I had under thirty days left; I made a full page calendar to check off the days. Sometimes I would cheat, mark three or four days off just so I could get closer to being with her. She would send me new pictures weekly and that was a blessing. I loved her dearly for that.

The Pastor came in our suite and I was telling him about the signs in the Bible about Morning Star and he said; *"If it's real, you'll get another one!"*

Then I asked if he had anything I could read and gave me a motivational book for the first three months of the year. When he left I picked it up and thought to myself I wonder what it says for my out date of February 2nd?

I opened it up to February 2nd and it said; *"The morning star rises in your heart?"* I screamed, everyone is like what, what, what happened! I told them, one inmate said; "If I hear the word Morning Star any more I'm going to shoot myself!"

In her last letter, she would be there to pick me up on my out date. That she would know from our first kiss!

I think the entire jail including the guards thought she was my dove after that. The day finally came, it was my out date; I get to leave at midnight. On your last day you don't have to work, but Sherry was working so I wanted to tell her goodbye.

At the end of the day, we were all on the line getting trays ready to send out to the prisoners, then one of the young kids says; "I'm going to miss you Kyle, you're the nicest man I've ever met!"

Then they all said, the same thing and Sherry said; "He is the nicest man, I've ever met, I'm going to miss him too, but I don't want to see you back in here."

When I left the kitchen, I was walking on cloud nine. I had six hours to go, Morning Star would be here to pick me up, and I wanted to hold her in my arms terribly because I was falling in love with her.

I gave all my belongings away, had my bags packed, and I was ready to go! Tick tock, tick tock, the longest hours of my life and then you don't know if they're going to let you out at midnight!

Then the high security doors flew open, I'm Free! Free at last! I got out of my sexy orange convict outfit, and back into my street clothes. The doors were clicking in front of me. I couldn't open them fast enough, to get to the lobby where my dove was patiently waiting for me.

Chapter Nineteen

HIGHER POWER

Sometimes you just wonder what's going on, I learned everything that happens under the sun is influenced by a higher power. The Lord brought Morning Star into my life at Christmas. I believe because of my love for the Holidays.

When I walked into the lobby my dove was fast asleep in a chair, I gently woke her up and said; *"It's so nice to see you Morning Star"*, we hugged each other, I walked out the door to freedom.

We went to her house, she offered to cook me dinner, but I settled for a salad because she wasn't feeling well, and wanted to rest. I told her no worries honey, lay down, I'll be fine.

I spent three days at her house; she wanted me to meet her family. Her son told me; "my mom likes you a lot," he and I hit it off right away. I had to go to probation the next day; the probation officer that put me in jail, and violated my civil rights, wouldn't even see me. He turned me over to someone else and then they just transferred me to a new County.

Morning Star and I went out for dinner that night; I went back to my house because I had a ton of things to get done. We made plans to go out on Valentine's Day. I went shopping and bought her a cute cuddly white teddy bear, so every time she hugged it, she would remember me.

She was going to meet me at my house around six o'clock, but didn't show up for a few more hours. I immediately sensed something very different about her but we still went out. She was very distant at dinner like she had a million thoughts going through her mind. Afterwards we stopped at my brothers for a minute. I told her why don't we make it an early night and we went back to my house! When she left I hugged her goodbye.

I didn't hear from her for a week, so I called and left her a message. She called me back, and said; "she went back with her boyfriend!" I told her I figured that on Valentine's Day, it's not a problem. I wished her the best, and there is no need to explain. Signs are very real. That's where free will comes in, free will, changes the course of your divine destiny.

I got a letter from the inmates in jail, and they all wanted to know if I "Fornicated" with my dove. I wrote them back and said; "No". I slept on the sofa at her house. I never once looked at her as a sexual object, or lusted after her, but had the greatest respect for her as a woman.

I never called or talked to her after that day. The last thing in the world I would do is get in the way of someone trying to work out a relationship. I loved her, and wanted her to be happy whatever her decision was in life.

Don't get me wrong, a day didn't go by, I didn't think about her. I got another motivational scripture book, laid down to read it. I opened it, and the first page I came too said; *"Morning star rises in your Heart!"* Imagine that!

The signs were overwhelming at times; they are still there if I look for them. It's been three months since I've talked to her; it's her birthday this week. I found a nice card that talked about friendship, thanked her for being there for me and motivating me.

That door closed on me and Morning Star on Valentine's Day. The signs were real, never ending. No matter how hard I hoped that she was my dove, free will came in, and it changed our destiny. I still would have liked to have had that kiss!

I can say with all honesty, after what she did for me, I would have devoted my heart, and soul to her for the rest of my life. I would have made it my life goal to make her the happiest woman in the world. That's how much I fell in love with her. But the doors were gently closed.

With my faith I struggled to find answers more so for myself if I could come up with one. God will give us signs and always back them up with scripture, he also gives us "free will" and that's when we make mistakes doing it on our own.

Nevertheless, the signs were never ending around Morning Star. She kept coming up roses! She gave me a deck of cards. I would think of her, walk by the cards, cut them and say; if the Ace of Spades comes up, she loves me, and every time I'd cut the deck the Ace of Spades came up.

I said; that's enough of cutting cards, because the Ace of Spades always came up. I walked outside, and moved a box in the garage, there was a piece of wood on the floor. I picked it up, turned it over, and it was an Ace of Spades. I quit cutting the cards and stopped looking for signs after that day.

The answer was; God brought Morning Star into my life when I needed Love. Between her and Sherry they both gave me the answers I was searching for. They both told me to save my girls, go after them no matter what, and never stop fighting for them. They're being deceived and you need to get them away from that woman.

Is everything you do by chance, or does it come from a higher power? I look at my life and everything I've always wanted to do come true! Was it luck or did I have the favor of the Lord with me all my life?

Maybe; but one thing for sure I've always tried to make a difference in the lives of other people I met in my travels. I think that alone is why the Lord has blessed me on my journey.

Way too many things have happened in my life that can only come from a higher power.

I've been declared dead, shot at more than once, stabbed, and came close to drowning multiple times, wrongfully imprisoned and lost everything I've owned. No matter what happened in my life; *'What I Learned Under the Sun'*, is I always come out smelling like a rose!

Anytime you force a door open, thinking you're going to get your way, ultimately you will regret it down the road. When the door of opportunity is shut, it is to lead us through a better door with greater opportunities.

'What I Learned Under the Sun', is we encounter a situation that appears hopeless, totally beyond our ability to handle; then God removes one obstacle after another, most of which we cannot explain, as we enjoy remarkable success.

Chapter Twenty

THE POWER OF THE LORD; "JUSTICE"

It's been almost a year and a half, and I was finally going to get my day in court, after being locked up for most of that time because of my ex-wife's deception! I just got out of jail and the FOC issued another Show Cause for Support against me.

It's like the FOC, by the direction of my ex-wife, knows when I'm about to be released and they get me back in court before I can even hire a lawyer. It's worked twice for them in the past. I couldn't get on the phone fast enough to hire a lawyer.

When I met with my lawyer he couldn't believe what has happened to me. My lawyer said; because of the fraud that my wife and her lawyer committed we'd have no problem winning the case. My lawyer was going to get a hearing as soon as possible, on these new felony support charges against me, my ex-wife's third attempt at putting me away.

How wicked is she; a week after I got out of jail after being locked up that seemed like forever, she filed another contempt charge against me, to get me locked back up again. Thank God I still had that twenty-two-thousand-dollar check in my wallet, to hire a lawyer, or my ex-wife would have gotten away with it, and put me back in jail for the third time.

Now, I'm not feeling the Love, I'm thinking someone should put her in jail and see how she likes it! Like Marlene said; from the beginning, "*My girls will never know what I've done*", like her other famous line, "walk-away or I'll put you away!"

'*What Marlene needs to Learn Under the Sun*', is they aren't HER girls, they are OUR girls, and always will be.

My lawyer went to the court house, got a court date then called me at home, and said; *"The **BIG** problem you have is you've got a Police Officer of Authority from Hesperia calling officials in the court telling them to believe everything Marlene says!"* Everyone in the court system is judging you, based on what your ex-wife tells them.

I wasn't surprised. Marlene has a history of using people in Authority to get what she wants. I've never in my life heard of a Police Officer getting personally involved in a woman's divorce case. That just seems a little fishy to say the least, but she does give him free drinks at the bars she works at.

But you have to admit, it's a brilliant strategy, pre-planning a divorce, and having a Police Officer of Authority back you up telling everyone in the court system that whatever Marlene say's is true! It might have been a nice strategy they cooked up in the bars, should be interesting to see how that turns out.

We finally got to court. In court transcript: my ex-wife said; "he had no desire to visit his kids, he says; they are the most disrespectful bitches that he had ever met." He didn't want them, he didn't want anything to do with them and then he went into rehab.

My lawyer: "Your Honor, he called for his kids, we have phone records to prove it. My client would really like to see his kids." My ex-wife then stated: *"I would suggest that it be supervised, because the minute they lay sight on him they are going to run screaming."*

The final outcome in court today: The court dropped the felony support charges and threw out the divorce because of the fraud committed by my ex-wife and her lawyer.

The Court ordered; a new divorce proceeding. Our first Court order was to go to mediation and solve our issues on property settlement and custody of my girls.

Two weeks later we were at mediation and it only lasted a few minutes. I offered my soon-to-be ex-wife the house, basically everything, and all I wanted was to see my girls. Then Marlene told the mediator; *"Sucks to be him, I already have everything!"*

Then out of the blue, Marlene says; *"What, is he going to write a book about all my affairs?"* "He can't even spel?"

The mediator said; "It's obvious this mediation isn't going to work with her attitude. We'll have to let the court decide the outcome and someone isn't going to like the ending."

As I walked out, the mediator wished me luck in court; I smiled and thanked him, then told him I'm not worried; *"I have the power of the Lord behind me!"* My ex-wife laughed as I walked out the door.

I was walking down the hall, turned the corner, her boyfriend was sitting there laughing at me and said; "Bring it on big boy!" I thought wow; they are a match made for each other.

I'm not talking a match-made-in-heaven. Make no mistake about it, their relationship will never be ordained by God, and it will never work out!

It never fails to amaze me, every time Charlie says; *"Bring it on big boy!"* It never works out for my wife—disaster soon follows her. Talk about blinded by sin. The Lord give's her sign, after sign, about what she's doing wrong, and she continues in it.

Well the next week in court, we; *"Brought it on!"* The Judge tossed out the divorce because it was illegal, because of the fraud my ex-wife and her lawyer committed. The judge turned to my ex-wife and looked at Charlie and said; *"I hope you're not married to that man?"* I turned and looked at Charlie and laughed. By the look on the "big man's" face, if he could have walked out of there like a mouse, he would have.

When I was in college, my ex-wife and her lawyer submitted a Divorce Judgment under the 7-day rule, two weeks before my scheduled pretrial conference, two and half weeks before my Divorce hearing. The court defrauded me and violated rules of civil procedure.

The court admitted that what they had done in transcripts was fraudulent! Then the Judge says; that there have been procedural irregularities here, that he kind of mucked it up, "So what"? Then the court admits I'm entitled to sanctions because of what happened. I'm not worried about me; I'm worried about the damage it caused our daughters.

The court ordered that the FOC Support Charges is otherwise, discharged, null and void because of the fraud. The Judge ruled that all child support arrearages attributable to Defendant are vacated and set aside, entirely. My wife tried to contest the ruling, but the Judge left it standing.

Pretty sad that the FOC can put you in jail for contempt of court on support arrearages, when you were never behind in support and never had a Divorce hearing for custody. They just lock you up and throw the key away. The Judge should have tossed the both of them in jail on the spot, because of the fraud they committed against me.

Then again, if he would have done that, I would have begged the Judge not to put my daughter's mother in Jail. That's not showing love and compassion to your spouse, and I would never want my girls to go through the embarrassment of their mom being in Jail. I actually felt bad for Marlene that she was ordered to pay me sanctions by the Judge.

My wife's fraud in the divorce was an illegal divorce, please! If you don't think the Lord didn't have his hands in that outcome, you're sadly mistaken; it just doesn't happen.

'What I Learned Under the Sun', is everything that happens under the sun happens for a reason. Guess what, now I'm married to her again! All I can say is; "Holy Smokes!"

My wife was right. I can't spel. I didn't want the divorce, I contested it, and my girls hated it, and God hated it. My wife pushed it to the limit with wickedness beyond comprehension. For the sake of the girls I would have done anything, even showed my wife compassion, forgiveness, and tried to work it out for the sake of OUR daughters.

Our second divorce hearing is about a month away and my wife's lawyer just dropped her like a hot potato, because of the fraud they committed in court! That should have been another sign for Marlene, to truly evaluate her present situation but as brilliant as she is; she took the advice of her bar friends, ran to another lawyer for advice.

My wife was pushing and demanding the court, to put me in prison for felony support. For some reason my wife wanted me out of the picture. It came to light during the discovery process that my wife had serious problems misappropriating the family savings, and committed six years of unorthodox tax filings. Then her lawyer tried to put the entire debt onto me in the illegal divorce judgment.

Now I'm thinking the only reason she wanted the Divorce was to hide her unorthodox tax filing ways, in desperation, get a Divorce, putting all the family debt onto me so she would be free and clear of any obligations to the State of Michigan and the IRS under her married name.

Why would I think that; maybe because she tried to get an annulment in Las Vegas where we got married, so she could get her name changed back into her maiden name, thinking it would clear her of any future criminal investigations from the State of Michigan and the IRS.

I guess her wise counselors in the bar, forgot to mention that they still go by her social security number, and she would still be responsible for debts owed the State of Michigan and the IRS even if she changed her name.

That is the beauty of forgiveness, if only Marlene would have come clean, with the power of the Lord we could have resolved any problems, or any secret financial issues going on in her life. Marlene elected to deceive herself, pass the blame onto me and try to cover it up.

I was beyond myself when I found out through the course of discovery what she had done, specially her unorthodox tax filings. During discovery my lawyer asked; my wife if she was having any sexual liaisons with anyone. My wife is probably the only woman in the world that would say "yes" going into a Divorce. She even, proudly wrote down the guys name and address for my lawyer, and then she stated in court, the affair had been going on for a year and a half.

My lawyer said; since she admitted to adultery in the marriage I would get half the estate, possibly custody if not at least joint custody.

Chapter Twenty One

GOD'S WILL ALWAYS PREVAILS

Finally I had my lawyer in place for my second divorce proceedings with my wife. He put the ball in motion to seek true justice, after we received our discovery documents from my wife. This made for some very interesting reading and showed a very clear picture what she was doing and why.

How do I address Marlene now? As my ex-wife or wife, since I'm not Divorced anymore. I guess, I'll go back to; "My loving Wife."

When I left his office today, I prayed to God I hope I'm doing the right thing and please give me some kind of sign, that this is the right decision I've made.

That afternoon Wayne called me, the guy that I was in jail with and invited me to go to church with him and his wife. I said; *"Yes, I'd love to."*

The church was in Newaygo, Michigan, I got there early, and was buying a cup of coffee. I felt an overwhelming presence behind me, and turned around to find my daughter Skyler standing beside me and staring at me.

She looked like she had a lot of sadness in her eyes and she just wanted to be close to her daddy since her mom had kept us apart for so long.

I was in awe, shocked and overwhelmed with joy. I said; *"Honey, how are you doing?"* and she smiled and said; *"Good"* and I saw those eyes turn to overwhelming joy, yet I could feel in her heart, she was very confused and had a million questions for me.

After seeing my daughter, I was more outraged at the court system for allowing Marlene to make false accusations against me, not taking any action to investigate it, but then if you have a Police Officer of Authority backing up your wife, it's no wonder no one did anything.

It was just horrible, what Marlene was putting our daughters through.

I just thank the Lord I had my entire family to support me. Ironically, the sermon was about sin and if you're living the life of sin you are of the Devil!

I didn't want to combat evil with evil, I just wanted my girls. My lawyer said; *"You can't be a nice guy when you're going up against a woman like that!"*

I thought about making Marlene one last offer for the sake of our girls. So I thought long and hard, and came up with a proposition for her, which I was sure she wouldn't refuse. I was going to have compassion for her, show her grace, and true love through forgiveness.

I walked into court and she had her boyfriend with her again. When Marlene saw me, she put her legs over Charlie, started hugging on him in front of me, and when she bent over to kiss him, I had to bite my tongue, when I saw her sporting a new tattoo on her rear-end.

I would have forgiven her for the affairs, but she went out and got a tattoo for Charlie, on her rear-end. I had to walk around the corner so she didn't see me laughing.

The offer I was going to hand her, I stuck back in my briefcase. That was about the only thing in the world she could have done, that I would have disowned her for is getting a tattoo for another man—GAME OVER!

He's a lucky man; I can tell he has a bright future with my wife. When she said to me; "that Charlie, can buy me over and over". I hope he has deep pockets, because he's going to need it in the future with her. I can only pray that he stands beside his woman no matter what the future brings them.

They finally called us into court for our *"second"* divorce hearing. My lawyer ordered a drug test on my wife before the custody hearing and she failed it. According to the Family Court Judge it was no big deal.

My wife told the Judge that if I got custody of my girls; they would commit suicide, that my entire family is psychotic! No one in my family is taking mind altering drugs from any physicians.

During the trial I watched in horror the evil flowing out of my wife, as her lips moved. I was blown away by the endless lies that came out of her mouth.

I had multiple professional witnesses present and none of them were allowed to testify on my children's behalf. My niece Shilo was present and she went into the restroom, while Marlene and I were in court, my girls were in there crying their eye's out.

Marlene's heart was so hardened; she had no clue what she was doing to our children. I didn't have to see the tears from our girls; I felt them in my heart.

My wife admitted to adultery and this Judge even reserved her Alimony and said; "I don't want to see Marlene pay anything." Then I was awarded half of the material property but I could only take inventory.

In court the Judge refused to acknowledge my tax return as income and wanted to add my losses in Las Vegas as earnings, and award my wife half. My lawyer said to the Judge, "I don't care if the man won a million dollars, she isn't entitled to it."

The Judge went on and said; "I had no right to hide it from Marlene." Holy smokes, she's having an affair, locks me out of the house and I owe her! The Judge starts talking about a barber who cuts hair for two dollars and socking away a dollar in the back yard so his wife didn't get it.

I'm like, this Judge is unbelievable; I went to Las Vegas with five thousand dollars and came home with seven thousand dollars, and then gave it to my wife towards child support. Then I'm supposed to give her half of my losses ~ wow! This Judge thinks I buried the money in the back yard under the bushes next to the fence.

I felt an Honorable Judge should have investigated my wife's horrible allocations, and he would have allowed my witnesses to testify, when my wife failed a drug test ~ the Judge should have looked into my wife's lifestyle. She was taking medication for crazy pills, lives her life in a bar seven nights a week and this Judge felt we should get joint custody, with primary physical custody to the mother, and the father can have supervised visits, because Marlene recommended that to the Judge.

Marlene and Charlie were celebrating in the court room, what they didn't understand or were clueless about, was that nobody won in court today, and my girls lost everything. They're the ones that will pay the price for the rest of their lives. Then again you really can't blame the Judge, he's been deceived by my wife and a Police Officer of Authority.

My wife was right when she said; *"I'm a wicked bitch!"* Someone should have told her about; *"What you sow, you will also reap,"* that your wickedness comes back onto you in this lifetime. No one can be that *"wicked"* and get away with it, the Bible is very clear that your wickedness will come back on you.

In the second divorce, I was awarded sanctions for the fraud committed against me in the first divorce. I'm having a hard time writing this while going through so many divorces from the same woman. I'm thinking, *"Holy smokes."* I must have missed the second marriage and totally missed the honeymoon. Marlene just went from my *"loving wife"* back to my ex-wife! Dang, can't believe I missed the honeymoon.

I thought the first divorce of five pages was evil. It wasn't anything compared to the second divorce of thirteen pages. My ex-wife's lawyer awarded the sanctions to my lawyer so I guess what she, sowed, she is already reaping. I assure you he filed paperwork immediately on her to get that money. I myself would have never made my ex-wife pay a penny.

True justice is showing compassion, mercy and forgiveness and I was about to show that to my ex-wife. Marlene was ordered to pay half the debt, it was a proven fact my ex-wife had serious problems misappropriating the family savings, and committed six years of unorthodox tax filings.

My wife never sent our taxes in that were done when we filed married jointly, except in another State I worked in. She would get the checks and cash them. Then she went out and hired another accountant, filed single head of household to get back more money in Michigan and five years of large sums from the IRS that I knew nothing about.

I was blown away by her unorthodox tax filings. It took me months to compile all the evidence from two different States, and copies of her cashed tax checks with only her name on them. I then had to go to our accountant and get five years of copies of returns. Before I could get them, I had to cover an eight hundred dollar check she bounced with the accounting firm.

Everyday it's amazing what I'm finding out that's gone on before Marlene's Divorce; things I never knew about. I wonder to myself, how she ever managed to hide all this craziness from me.

To save her butt, I would have to go back five years, file single, and assume the entire tax debt. I don't hate my wife, never have, just hated when she had affairs on me!

I was willing to show her compassion but not at the cost of her keeping my daughters hostage. I still haven't seen my girls.

When I got home from court after our second Divorce, I called my now ex-wife and left her a message; "If you bring my daughters over to see my family, I will show you compassion and mercy today and save you from possible future criminal investigations from the State of Michigan and the IRS.

I called again a week later at the bar and a man answered and said; "sucks to be you, Marlene got everything!" I'm sure it was Charlie and his remark just cost his lover big time. I'm glad he's got deep pockets when they look into her accounting practices and red flag her for life, she will need an old guy with deep pockets.

I thought, "Sucks to be me!" I took all the evidence, got on the first plane to Kansas City, Missouri, to meet with the IRS. They fixed my taxes on the spot because of the unorthodox tax filings my wife committed. I'm sure some day she'll wish she would have taken my offer of compassion, and let me see my daughters.

I'm all for showing my ex-wife compassion and mercy but not at any cost, if she keeps my daughters held hostage and won't let me see them.

Sometimes you don't know it at the time, but she turned so far into sin that the Lord had other plans for me; it wasn't to be with my ex-wife. On this day 9-9-9 she was granted her second Divorce and changed the lives of her daughters forever. We were married sixteen years to the day. Think about that for a minute, we were married sixteen years to the day!

Humans say; "All's fair in Love and War." Adultery is a sin, no matter how hard you try to justify your actions in your own mind; one day you will answer for it.

'What I Learned Under the Sun', is Divorce is just plain evil, now I know why God hates it! My ex-wife said; I can't spel. It's not the

spelling; it's trying to put this unbelievable true story on paper, and try to make some sense out of it. That's the hard part!

One should learn; "There's Good and Evil" and "Heaven and Hell". As humans we have the gift of free will and sometimes tend to forget that the gate into heaven is a narrow one.

The Lord gave me the vision on what my Journey in life was to be through Deuteronomy 27, and I was finally done in court, I hope. Now I can move on full speed ahead. I assure you Gods going to open all the right doors for me at lightning speed, now that I've been set free from my ex-wife.

My story is about "Faith cannot be trusted until it has been tested." My faith has been tested and *"You have to have faith even against seemingly insurmountable odds."*

Chapter Twenty Two

WHEN THE TRUTH IS UNBELIEVABLE

I always thought the whole divorce was about her affairs, I was dead wrong. It was about addiction, deception and unorthodox tax filings. Now that the divorce was behind me I filed a motion in court today, to "terminate my probation" because my Probation Officer violated my civil rights and due process.

About three weeks later I went to court. As I was sitting in the court room for my hearing before a different Honorable Judge, the Prosecutor walked up, handed me a paper that states; the court denied the defendant's motion to terminate his probation.

I thought, *"Holy smokes, not again!"* Then just before my hearing everyone disappears in like seven different directions. The new Honorable Judge called me up, even before I got to the bench he states; I read your motion word for word Mr. Coon and as of today you're off of probation.

Then when I left this judge told me next time you go to Las Vegas I want to go with you! I guess he did read my motion, word for word.

A friend of mine is a Judge in another county; maybe I just might surprise the both of them one day. I guess when my book comes out; I'll take both of them a signed copy, they might want to skip, right to the chapter on Las Vegas. Who knows, what those pages might hold, when they open the book.

Wow; I almost drifted off there and was actually ready to catch a flight. But my girls have become a statistic to the Friend of the Court system. With all the evidence I compiled, I made it my mission to get justice for my daughters.

Joint custody doesn't mean anything, when your ex-wife is holding your kids hostage, over twenty two thousand dollars in *"my"* travel expense reimbursements, she thought she was entitled to.

'*What I learned Under the Sun*', is it was a true blessing, Marlene didn't go to Las Vegas with me, and I didn't give her the money. It took every penny to pay legal fees or she would have succeeded with her evil plan of putting me back in jail the third time.

I purchased all the court transcripts and sent them to every agency in the State of Michigan that had anything to do with the FOC, the court system and anyone else I could think of to get justice for my girls. To investigate what happened in court violating my civil rights and due process, and what could be done about everyone involved with my ex-wife's crooked Divorce.

I turned over all the evidence to the State of Michigan Department of Human Services and Administrative Office Friend of the Court for the fraud that my ex-wife and her lawyer committed against me. I turned Marlene's lawyer into The Michigan Attorney Grievance Commission for lawyer misconduct. That is under investigation and they will make their ruling in six months.

I've spent thousands of dollars fighting for my daughters. When I started doing research on-line I was horrified of the stories I was reading about what the Friend of the Court has done to other loving parents and destroyed the lives of multitudes of children.

All I wanted was to see my girls. I've done everything possible under the sun to get them. I took all the court transcripts and compiled them into a short format of the Family Judge's comments during the divorce hearings and was personally astonished at how this judge conducted himself.

I have never seen a Judge so biased or prejudiced in court in my entire life let alone use such language as a lawman. Some of the language used by the Judge in court transcripts consists of: addressing my wife as "Marlee" her bar maid "nick name"; "bunny trail", "procedural irregularities", "mucked it up", "sizeable hunk to Marlee", "that's the way I'm going to jump", "Nah,nah,nah", "poor old mom" and regarding the fraudulent divorce ~ "So what". From the court transcripts it was obvious from day one that this Judge was for Marlene, she knew it, my lawyer knew it. Marlene knew it and laughed about it even in court, she knew from day one she would get everything, so I turned the Judge into the Judicial Tenure Commission.

The Friend of the Court Bureau contacted me and said, it was created to establish policies and procedures for the statewide operation of the child support system and does not have the authority to investigate or discipline a County (FOC) office. Only the director of that County FOC has direct oversight and the Judge of the County oversees the FOC.

Then they say; if you do not agree with the system, you have the option to appeal it and will be in your best interest to hire an attorney. So basically no one oversees the FOC system but the system itself and I'm supposed to spend thousands of more dollars fighting the system!

Thank the Lord I'm paid up in Support because it's an evil system.

The general public thinks the FOC is friendly and no one truly knows how evil the system is until your children become a statistic.

The laws should be simpler, if you want to commit adultery in the marriage, the other loving parent should get everything. My wife admitted to adultery in discovery and the courts gave her everything, and then praised her. I personally empathize with any man who wants to be a part of their children's lives but cannot because the mother stands in the way. This is child abuse.

In the end the Judge awarded my ex-wife everything she wanted. What blew my mind was at the last hearing when the Divorce was final. I received the signed Judgment of Divorce in the mail a few weeks later after court. It was signed by my wife and her lawyer a month before our final court hearing, making this Divorce Questionable.

It was very obvious the Judge already knew his decision and was giving everything to my ex-wife, no matter what. That told me I was in for the battle of my life to get my kids. There was no-way I was going to contest the second Divorce. I couldn't handle three Divorces from the same woman without a honeymoon.

Even after the Divorce the horror of my ex-wife's slander didn't end. One of Marlene's friends on Facebook posted slander on my page, and then sent the same evil messages to all my friends. Here is an insert from the message from: Mr. Way commented on your status; "you are using Facebook to market crap under the falsehood of religion. Furthermore, I will tell as many people on your friends' list as possible that you're a fake. He doesn't even know 600 people; you would be hard pressed to find 60 people that even like him, including the Law Enforcement in Hesperia Michigan."

After her Divorce, I'm thinking why is a friend of my ex-wife on my Facebook slandering me? This guy; falsehood of religion ~ wow! You are either of the light or you're of the darkness and if you're of the light people in the darkness will hate you.

I'm flattered that my ex-wife's friend is so worried about me. I'm wondering why a married man that lives in Florida has so much concern for my ex-wife in Michigan.

The irony of this; this guy befriended me, and was the one that told me not to call my wife, to give her time. So I never did, I only called for the girls. I guess the two of them spent one too many nights on the road together, doing shows and this is a guy I trusted.

Holy smokes, I guess you have to be very careful who you pick as a friend. I always wondered why that guy always came around the house without his wife!

'What I Learned Under the Sun', is that God will always give you a sign when you ask for one. I have also learned under the sun, that God will use other people to disclose to you what and why things are happening in your life. Nothing is hidden under the sun!

I look at this message from Mr. Way as a blessing in disguise. It sums up my entire case on something Mr. Way said; "Law Enforcement in Hesperia, Michigan." Very soon I would find out the meaning behind this message, talk about a sign!

You have to Love MARK 4:22 "For whatever is hidden is meant to be disclosed, and whatever is concealed is meant to be brought out into the open."

Chapter Twenty Three

ONE BREATH AWAY FROM ETERNITY

In the end you have to have faith even against seemingly insurmountable odds. The Lord will bless you beyond your wildest dreams. I can't emphasize that enough; you have to have faith and wait patiently for Him to show you the way.

No matter how bad it gets or how many doors are slammed in your face, have faith and He will open all the right doors for you. I never realized it, but He's closed a lot of doors in my life, and always opened the right doors when I needed them.

So many things happened in my life that the odds of them happening are so inconceivable that they could only have come from a Higher Power. That's; *'What I Learned Under the Sun'*.

The power of prayer is very real, and very powerful to this day! Be careful what you pray for because if you have faith; it'll be yours if you ask. You have to live by faith, when the Lord opens up doors for you, and gives you a sign; walk through it because that door will change your life forever! You just have to be patient, remember we're on His time.

What is true love? It's a lifelong process of commitment, sacrifice, enduring hardships, and we're all searching for that perfect love filled with passion and romance. In the end you find the answer, and it's within all our reaches, and you have to open your *"Heart"* to find it! You have to be sensitive to each other's needs like a dove!

My ex-wife invited Satan into our house, and destruction soon followed. I never lost faith, the Lord opened all the right doors, and positioned me to be more successful than I could have ever imagined.

'What I Learned Under the Sun', is all you have to do is keep the faith, and wait patiently, no matter what the problems are, everything works out in the end.

While my wife and I were in mediation in court, she made the statement about my faith. That I expect the family to sit in her front yard on their knees and scream, *"Oh Jesus"*! I thought, *"wow"*; she's missed the whole point on what having faith is.

I'm sure, there are a lot of Jesus freaks that do, that's awesome they're on fire for Jesus, I wish everyone was. On the other hand just as many people struggle to deal with Christianity and Religion. Everyone is their own person, and I think they have to find that out for themselves.

It's not about Christianity or Religion, it's about what's in your HEART; when you figure that out, you open the secret to receiving the Holy Spirit. It doesn't matter what church you attend or what your religion is. What matters is, if you're right with God, you walk in the Light and not the darkness.

I can assure you the ones that have the Holy Spirit come on them, their lives will change forever, and they will turn from their lifestyle of sin, destruction, and addictions. They will have a whole new life and live in the light.

I've met all kinds who claim to be Christians, but for the lust of greed would hurt you in a heartbeat! I've met pastors that were above helping people or giving someone the time of day if they see you on the streets. God is everywhere and He sees everything, not just within the four walls of a place to worship on Sundays.

Then you have the non-believers, atheists and pagans and everyone else under the sun.

'What I Learned Under the Sun', is it's all about love, it's within all of us, and it's in your HEART. That is the secret under the sun; your

heart is the key and when you turn from sin, the Lord will soften your heart, and overwhelm you with the joy of the Holy Spirit.

'What I Learned Under the Sun', is when you praise God, that's when miracles start happening in your life. When the Holy Spirit comes on you, you don't turn into a freak. You are transformed in body, mind, and soul. You have very different values in life. You harbor no hatred for anyone, you know for the first time in your life what true love is.

For me, that is the beauty of my faith. I've learned the secret, the power that comes with it, and the overwhelming sensation of what true love is all about. I still have the same personality. I still look the same, but my heart isn't hardened anymore against anyone, whatever I do or speak comes from my heart, I have eyes and can see again.

People living in sin, have no idea they are sinning, see nothing wrong with it; it's only a new age to them. They're usually selfish, self-centered; full of pride, and everything is about them!

Heaven and hell is a very real place. You just don't know how much time you have here before your next adventure starts. I pray everyone would come to the light and be saved. Can you look in the mirror in the morning and say; praise God and give thanks for another beautiful day? "The answer is in your heart", look in the mirror with your heart, you will see the most beautiful person in the world.

I'm actually a thousand percent different in many ways inside that people in the light can only see. People just see the nicest person they've ever met. One that's always happy. And that is what it's all about; happiness, joy, and overwhelming love.

I've always had it but never knew the power that came with it! I've never worried about anything in my life. No matter what problems that's in your life, everything will work out in the end.

That is the whole point of having faith! No matter how many problems you face daily; separation, divorce, loss of job, loss of a loved one, monetary hardships or home foreclosed, no matter what your problem is; if you have faith, turn from your life of sin, pray, and read the Bible the Lord will take all your problems away, open more doors for you than you could ever imagine.

Never give up faith. No matter how hard times get you will always come out on top for the better than the present situation you're in. God uses everything that happens in your life all for His Glory under the sun. Keep the faith, you won't be let down!

My entire lifelong dream was to have a nice house on a lake, help people in need, travel, and enjoy life to the fullest. By waiting patiently and praying the Lord has opened up the doors of opportunity for me and blessed me more than I could ever imagine. He put me back on the right track, has big plans for my future, and my daughters. I have the faith, He won't let me down!

I have incorporated "One Breath Away,™" because no matter what I do, I always get another sign, and pull right back to the idea I received from a vision while reading Deuteronomy 27. I've set a store page up for protection of the name, until I'm in a position to move forward. When I ask for a sign, miraculously I always get one. I'm pretty positive that "One Breath Away™" is part of my future.

It's been a few years since the major scripture signs at church and I just know when you ask for a *"sign"* you get one. So I felt the need to ask; the next morning I walked outside and there is a piece of paper wadded up on the ground. I open it up, and it read "Jesus Saves, legend of the dogwood tree story" and then checked "Promise of God". I thought "wow", talk about a sign for "One Breath Away™" and for what is going on in my life.

The company I founded, "One Breath Away™" is all about the Cross and the Oaks of Righteousness, and helping people in need. I found this wadded up paper in my yard that says, "Promise of God," I go to the website and I'm blown away in awe, it's all about Jesus, Court, Government and Righteousness through the cross.

My closest neighbors are at least a hundred yards away. I know they didn't print that piece of paper and put it at the front of my door. I pretty much know what my future plans are, and its revolved around the Cross and "One Breath Away ™".

After I got through all that craziness with my ex-wife and multiple divorces, having to decide on what my new career was going to be entered my mind. All my friends told me I should write a book, virtually everyone I met said; *"You should write a book"*. The signs were never ending for me to write a book.

'What I Learned Under the Sun', is when you get a sign from the Lord nothing is impossible. Soon, I will open "One Breath Away™", Christian Retail Store, so there is no sense in trying to fight it if it's my destiny.

The International Christian Retail Show was coming up in Denver. All the publishers would be there. I knew I had to go as it was part of my future. Anyone that travels in our family my mom always makes them chocolate chip cookies for the road. I didn't want any, and she made me take some anyways. I flew out of Muskegon to Detroit, Michigan, then on to Denver, Colorado for the show.

While in Detroit, I was eating in a restaurant next to a window. A group of blind people went by, I quickly breathed said a prayer for them; that they would make it safely to their gate and have a safe flight.

Half an hour later I made my way to my gate, when I got there, the group of blind people I prayed for were sitting there. They were sitting by themselves, I guess no one wanted to sit by them. So, I sat in the middle of them and started a conversation. One girl in the group said she was hungry so I got out my mom's cookies and gave them all to the group.

Then they started to board the flight to Denver, I just hung back until last, when I boarded the ticket agent looked at my ticket and said; *"I've got a better seat for you!"* She bumped me up to First Class, I thought; *"cool"*. Now tell me that isn't a blessing from God. What are the chances of praying for a group of blind people, and they're at your gate, when there are hundreds of gates in the Detroit Airport.

It was probably the most relaxed flight I've ever been on in my life. I knew that it was a blessed flight and I also knew my trip would be blessed.

On the first morning of the show, there was a woman outside with tons of luggage and I asked her if she needed any help. She said; *"Are you sure you don't mind?"* I said; "Not a problem I can carry everything". She had lots of luggage and it weighed a ton. She held the door for me. She told me she had to go way on the other side of the convention center to a room.

When we got there she thanked me and told me the Lord told her to bless me with an interview. I said; "for what?" She said; "for your book!" Holy smokes, talk about a sign. I asked her when and she said in twenty minutes after she gets set up. This truly blew my mind. I don't even have a book out yet and I'm doing an interview on a Christian TV show.

When I talk about signs and divine interventions it doesn't get any better than what happened in Denver. Sometimes you can get very excited when you have eyes that can see and start seeing signs.

So, I don't think it was by chance what has happened in my life and I am pretty positive I'm writing this book for a reason. I believe signs and numbers. They are very real including my marriage and divorce date. We were married on September 9th and both our daughters were born on the 9th that equals 9-9-9. The day of my wife's divorce is 9-9-9, all of those things have meanings.

What are the odds of going through a fraudulent Divorce, the court tossing it out, and having to get Divorced again, then after all the court hearings, the final day for your Divorce, just happens to fall on September 9th, sixteen years to the day you got married.

I truly believe numbers are very powerful. *'What I Learned Under the Sun'*, is when you have eyes that can see and a heart for God, you will know the meaning under the sun! Nothing is ever what it seems to be and nothing is impossible, if you have faith under the sun.

I know if Marlene would have had faith; her life would have been blessings on top of blessings on this date of 9-9-9, but through her evil, she altered her destiny on a day of a major blessing. With her actions, she reversed her destiny and her number flipped flopped to 6-6-6 the mark of the beast. She used free will; it changed the course of her destiny and her life forever. *'What I Learned Under the Sun'*, is everything happens for a reason and nothing is hidden under the Sun!

I can assure you the date 10-10-10 is going to be special for me, as well as my daughters. I believe that's the start date, there will be miracles on top of miracles happening in my life and I'm looking forward to that day now that I've been set FREE. My ship will come in.

Chapter Twenty Four

DESTINY; MOUNTAINS ARE MOVED AND THINGS HAPPEN AT LIGHTNING SPEED

I never thought in a million years that my ex-wife wouldn't come to her senses and return back to God. I was even more overwhelmed at how many of my friends told me they had prayed for Marlene to quit the bar life.

The beauty of free will, you can actually alter your destiny by listening to other people, thus making the wrong decisions in life that will change the course of your destiny in life.

'What I Learned Under the Sun', is that true faith is the ability to believe and trust in God in the midst of suffering. Wait patiently for Him, pray, and then believe in a miracle to happen in your life and it will.

I'm sure with a 50% divorce rate, a lot of couples' stories are probably the same, just a change in characters, place, and time. We all have trials and tribulations. We are conquerors, and through our faith come out on top—always!!!

'What I Learned Under the Sun', is faith cannot be trusted until it has been tested. My faith was tested many times and "you have to have faith even against seemingly insurmountable odds."

'What I Learned Under the Sun', is God uses people for His purpose in many ways. He knew He could use me because of my strength and faith. One of the major characteristics of a God-ordained testimony is for something to happen that cannot be explained in the natural. In

other words, if you can make it happen through your abilities, it is not a testimony about God, but about you.

Trying to sort this whole mess out, with my ex-wife was overwhelming, but in the end it wasn't about her or our divorce at all. You see we are to pray for people that God puts in positions of Authority, and He allows "one" to hold such an Honorable Position in life. But when you abuse your "power" God will also put the right people in place to have you removed.

It only took four words from a Police Officer of Authority to bring a MAJOR investigation onto an entire Court System, and that was; *"Believe everything Marlene says!"*

The Lord gave me the strength and power to endure the evil, along with the wisdom to compile all the evidence, and get it to the right Commissions and Agency's for investigations. No one's going to hold my girls hostage, I sent massive documents to every State Agency that had anything to do with my daughters and anyone that could help them, even after I was strongly **WARNED** by a court official not to take this "Outside the County."

Make no mistake about it, one day God will deliver my daughters to me. He's not going to let my ex-wife hold them hostage much longer. I'm sure when the smoke clears from all these investigations someone's not going to be happy.

I prayed and asked God "what I was supposed to do," and the next morning I received an e-mail from an old associate and he said; *"You're a remarkable salesperson, Kyle,"* right out of the blue, I haven't talked to this guy in over five years.

The Lord always gives me a sign when I ask; but for me the answers come through other people, places, words and even crumpled papers. Here I am now and my past sales record pretty much says it, doing over a hundred million in sales for other people in my life.

So I figured from all the signs, it's my turn now. That's why I personally elected to self publish this book because of my vast expertise in selling to every major chain store. I'm not worried about anything, if it's meant to be it will happen!

My next e-mail was from an old buyer friend who asked me if my book was done yet, that's he's the new book buyer now and thought about me. Talk about a sign on what I should be doing, doesn't get any clearer than that. Literally overnight everything that was lost or taken from me could be restored. Pretty much like the final chapter of JOB in the Bible.

This is a "New Season" . . . Expect the unexpected this year . . . . I'm sensing there will be many great surprises! I can just feel it in the air that another miracle is going to happen anytime, maybe not for me; *"But for you."*

The Bible is very powerful. I've learned no matter what doors are closed, and at the time you don't understand it, just be patient, He will open more doors of opportunity for you that you couldn't have imagined that will take you to your destiny under the sun.

'What I Learned Under the Sun', is that no matter how bad things get, never, never give up and keep the faith. In no time at all, miracles will start happening in your life. Follow your heart, search out your dreams; anything can be accomplished under the sun!

I guarantee you everything I've lost to my ex-wife will be restored a thousand fold, and I'll come out with another book called: *"What I Did Under the Sun©"* This book will be about how I did it, the outcome of my daughters' situation, and what happened in the court system from all the investigations and what I did with "One Breath Away™."

I went out and got the newspaper, and wasn't surprised to see that the headlines read: *"Hesperia Police Chief; 'I've been fired."* Today's headline news and I give credit to The Muskegon Chronicle for reporting that, "The Chief has no idea why he is being replaced, he says came out of the blue. The Chief stated, "I've never had a verbal reprimand. I'm at a loss about what's transpired."

Was the Power of the Lord at work today: God always prevails to you what's going on, like Mr. Way said, "Including the Hesperia Police Department." I know what transpired!

That's the power of the Lord and Justice does prevail in the end! If you are personally involved with a married woman's divorce, abuse your power of authority to sway the outcome of a divorce hearing for the sake of that woman, you missed one very important aspect.

The children you're damaging with your deception and lies *"Are God's Children."*

I thought this would be the third year I wouldn't see my girls for Christmas. To my surprise my ex-wife called on Christmas Eve and said; *"your girls want to stop by for only a minute!"* That's what I prayed for. I had bought cell phones for them, months earlier and took them to their school. They told me what they wanted for Christmas and I had everything wrapped and under the tree for my Angels.

I'm sure my girls bugged their mother to death to see me. When they got to my house they couldn't get in fast enough to be with me. One by one, the first thing both my daughter's did was take me into my bedroom away from their mother and hugged me.

Marlene wasn't going to hold my daughters hostage one more Christmas, my girls made sure of that!

That is what Christmas is all about. **Miracles!** My girls really didn't care about the gifts. They only wanted to see their dad and to know their dad loved them.

They saw their dream come true over the course of the next three hours at my house, my girls have never felt so loved, after being deceived by their mother that dad abandoned them! Guess what, the truth set them free, on Christmas Day they knew their dad loved them.

They also saw me extend that love towards their mother. I even bought her a Christmas present, a set of crystal glasses. I have no hatred for Marlene, when she walked in the door I handed her a cup of coffee to make her feel welcome.

When my girls left, they were the happiest girls in the world. My youngest got home and posted on her MySpace; *"Dude wow, awesome day wow, wow great time!"*

It was about the Holy Spirit on this Christmas Day, my girls saw the light and the love that their dad has for them. That my life was filled with Love, Joy and Happiness and my home was filled with that love the minute my daughters walked in the door.

Both my daughters found the secret under the sun on Christmas Day, and it comes from within your heart. Not from lies and deception from another parent that had been deceiving them for years. That's what Christmas is all about; *"Love,"* and the moment Paris and Skyler saw their dad they knew without a doubt that his love for them burned bright as ever!

Chapter Twenty Five
LEAVE NO ONE BEHIND

For the last three years my girls have been alienated from their father, and finally know that their dad loves them and did NOT leave them. It was a few months later my daughter Paris called, and asked if I could come and pick her up, that she wants to live with me. I said; *"sweetie I will do anything in the world for you, you never have to ask your dad, my door is always open for you, I will never leave you or forsake you."*

Then Paris said "Mom is going to go talk with the Judge in the morning to see if I can live with you." I said, "Honey your mom isn't going to do that."

What! Marlene's going to go court and tell the Judge she lied on the PPO that I abused my kids and they fear for their life! That's what started this nightmare custody hearing.

If Marlene had any love for our daughters she wouldn't have filed a false report in court claiming I abused our daughters, taking our girls from me. Because of her lies right from the beginning Marlene convinced the courts that I had to have supervised visits because if my daughters had to see me they would run screaming for their life, and they didn't want to be a statistic on the six o'clock news. I stayed in the marriage to protect our daughters from the mother.

It wasn't just me. Marlene has kept my daughters from my entire family the last three years. Everyone invites my girls but Marlene won't let them come around my family. She even went as far to write a horrifying statement against my entire family, so the courts wouldn't let my girls around any of them.

What Marlene was doing was mental murder! Marlene was alienating her ex-husband and his entire family trying to cover up her own wickedness, lies, and deception.

'What I Learned Under the Sun', is "Hatred is not an emotion that comes naturally to a child. It has to be taught. A parent who would teach her children to hate the other parent represents a grave and persistent danger to the mental and emotional health of that child."

Not only was Marlene abusing the system to alienate the children's father, but it was costing the girls many family vacations and not allowing the girls to come to any family birthday's, not even their own birthday parties, something she as a mother could never make up to our girls.

Last year on my girls' birthday's I wanted to fly them to Minneapolis to the Mall of America to celebrate their birthdays, and Marlene wouldn't let them go and blamed it on the court that the Judge wouldn't allow it.

Marlene uses the Judge telling our girls that it's entirely his fault, that's how she plays her deceptive games with our kids. It's not her fault, it's your dad's fault, it's the Judges fault, and it's the courts fault. It's everybody's fault but Marlene's.

I asked my youngest who just turned fourteen, if she wanted to go to Vegas with me on her birthday, and she said yes. So I asked Marlene if I could take both girls to Vegas on their birthdays, and of course she said "no" and blamed it on the court system again.

My daughters have traveled all over with me, I wanted to show them the Hoover Dam, the desert, and Vegas at Nighttime. Then walk to all the casinos, get them souvenirs, and cool pictures at some of the most magnificent attractions on earth. I especially wanted to take my daughter Paris to the "Paris Hotel" so she could buy some souvenirs with her name on them.

This was the third year of birthdays my ex-wife has taken away from our girls and has not allowed them to be with me or my family. My ex-wife's plan was to bury me, put me away, or get me to the point where I would leave the State, and *'just'* walk away!

She forgot one very "important" thing; *"I would never abandon my girls or ever leave them behind or walk away from them."* That's the biggest mistake my ex-wife made; thinking I would leave my girls behind and stop fighting for them.

The next day the FOC investigator called me and said, "Your wife is taking you back to court over support." Then she said, "We know you're paid up but you're giving a lot of money to your girls, that's what your support is for and it should go to Marlene."

She said "I have to agree with Marlene," if you give your daughters three hundred dollars for special dresses that is a little excessive, and spend a thousand dollars on them at Christmas. If you have that kind of money to give to your girls, it should be going to the mother. Then she said, "This isn't support and this money should be going to the mother for support."

When is this nightmare going to stop in the court system? It has to stop being about *"money"* and start being about what is the "best interest of the children!" I would have never guessed in a million years on how crazy a divorce could be. With my ex-wife it has nothing to do with the kids at all; but the *"money"*, the root of all evil.

So here is what we have, the investigator continued, "next Friday you will come into court and meet a Referee on the issues your ex-wife has with you giving money to your daughters." (Expletive); you pay support, you do more for your girls anytime they ask and the ex-wife takes you back to court because she wants more money.

I no more than got off the phone with the Friend of the Court and my daughter called and wants to stop in and see me. These are the girls that fear for their life and will commit suicide if they have to see their dad, according to their mom.

So my ex-wife has me back in court on support and the Referee triples my support (based on my potential earnings), and goes retroactive back two and a half years to my wife's affair, instantly putting me over twenty thousand dollars in arrears.

I just want to see my daughters and I have to keep fighting for my life with the FOC so my ex-wife can't put me in jail for the third time. So I immediately filed an Objection to the Referee findings.

I left court, stopped and grabbed a newspaper, got home opened it up, and about fell out of my chair. My ex-wife was in the news for her second drunk driving arrest.

No wonder my ex-wife wants me back in court for more money, not for the sake of my girls, could she possibly want to pay for her second Drunk Driving Arrest? It looks like her sowing is starting to come around her way. Does sowing come around? Absolutely, make no mistake about it!

I thought the Divorce was over. I almost forgot how *"dangerous"* of a woman Marlene was. I was outraged, she was trying to put me back in Jail, using and abusing the Justice System for her own means. Marlene is becoming like a bad dream, that won't go away.

Since my ex-wife is getting me back into court, I also filed a motion for termination of parental rights, because Marlene received another drunk driving violating a court order—no alcohol.

It's astonishing how much money her divorce has caused the family, especially our children. The only people who are getting the money are the lawyers, and the court system. Combine all our legal fees and court costs over the last three years, we could have bought both girls new cars for their birthday.

That's the sad reality, Marlene continues to give thousands of dollars to lawyers to keep me and my family from the girls, and then at every court hearing parade our poor innocent children into court with Charlie, like their some big happy family. I can't even comprehend any mother dragging their innocent children into court at every hearing and have them sit in the court hallway all day for show and tell.

We are in court every month, it never ends. At our next hearing we got to court and in the court room sitting near Marlene are two ferocious lions (her friends) from the FOC waiting to devour me, and the Judge ordered a full investigation, and set a new court date for June.

This was a special day like no other, my ex-wife lied to the judge constantly at this hearing. Thank God the Judge finally saw her deception, she still lied. After court I ordered the transcripts, and filed thirty subpoenas that would prove with a preponderance of evidence that my ex-wife was constantly lying in court. "Justice can only prevail based on the truth."

The judge set a court date and my ex-wife went behind his back, to her friends (ferocious lions) that works in the FOC and filed another motion against me for contempt for support in desperation to get me locked up for the third time.

Thank the Lord this Judge had wisdom to see through her evil and had it cancelled. At the last hearing the FOC Officer walked up and hugged my ex-wife and said; *"Don't worry honey, we'll get him."* That's pretty scary, when the FOC Enforcement Officer is out to get you.

My friend Sheri called me up in the morning, and said she saw my ex-wife in the bar drunk, obviously upset or depressed because the man she was going to marry dumped her. He found himself another Harley

Chick, one a lot younger and prettier! Wow; talk about sowing and reaping coming full circle.

That's standing beside your woman. At least Marlene still has his tattoo to remember him by. I guess she found out the hard way that the grass wasn't greener on the other side of the fence, but scorched with deception and deceit.

Come to find out Charlie, dumped her after her Divorce was final. The man she thought was worth committing adultery for, thought nothing of dumping her for another woman.

In a way you have to feel sorry for her, it's a hard lesson to learn when you turn from God. That's why God gives us free will and when you turn from Him it usually doesn't work out very well and Marlene's problems are far from over, with all the investigations going on.

I had a few months to get all the evidence together to prove my ex-wife an unfit mother so my family and I could see the girls. A few days later I go out to the mailbox, the evidence had started rolling in. Not only was I overwhelmed with what I found out, it blew my mind. I was beside myself, for the life of me I couldn't even comprehend why my ex-wife was so wicked.

So I did a background check on line with the Michigan and Florida State Police, when the results popped up on the computer screen I fell out of my chair, when I saw her criminal history. I guess I should have done a background check on her before I married her.

The evidence was overwhelming, my entire family experienced a wide range of emotions, including disbelief, sadness, frustration, helplessness, despair, and anger from what we found out what my ex-wife had done.

I found out my ex-wife had our oldest daughter institutionalized in a psychiatric hospital just before Christmas for a mental disorder.

The Hospital findings indicated my daughter had *"Posttraumatic Stress Disorder,"* disruption of family by divorce.

Soon after that incident, my daughter didn't even want to attend school anymore; "what kid would, after their mother had you institutionalized at fifteen years of age in a psychiatric hospital?" I can't even begin to express my feelings. I couldn't be there to protect my daughter from her mother. I felt so helpless.

My ex-wife has what appears to be *"Parent Alienation Syndrome."* Basically this is a mother, through verbal and non-verbal thoughts, actions and mannerisms, was deceiving my daughters, and emotionally abusing them (brainwashed) into thinking their father had abandoned them, was a deadbeat dad and making him the enemy in the divorce.

Marlene was so obsessed with reaching her goal that she literally destroyed her own daughters. Simply put, this is a "sickness", and any mother seeking to destroy the father by using her children, should be considered and unfit mother.

The court ordered both parents to have a Psychology Evaluation. My results were; *"Kyle, is a good man, with no substance abuse issues past or present, and with no domestic violence issues at all. Kyle, can be assumed to be a fine man who has been seriously emotionally traumatized by his ex-wife."* There is nothing she can do to me, it is what she doing to our children that's traumatizing!

Marlene found a Psychologist in another county, and his report was based on her and Charlie's responses. Insane, Marlene brought the old man in with her, and probably searched multiple counties to find someone that would listen to their stories.

I'm not a rocket scientist; but common sense for the courts would be to send both parents to the same Psychologist to find out the true issues the children are having, leaving the ex-boyfriend out of it.

My girls need both parents in their lives; one thing that I promised my daughters is I would never keep them from seeing their mom ~ ever! I told my daughters that I'm pretty positive after court they would be able to travel with dad.

Walking into court, I was on cloud nine knowing things should go the right way for the sake of our girls. There were too many things that I introduced to the court that by law should have made my request for custody of my girls an easy decision for anyone.

I wasn't seeking sole physical custody; I just wanted a normal custody judgment where both parents got to see the children. So my daughters could have a normal life and be with my family.

The last few years, especially the past few months were torture for me. I compiled evidence for my case, looked up laws and ordinances, filed motions, and did everything I could to save my daughters from a manipulative, destructive, and just plain mean woman.

Little did I know that the evils of a temptress reached farther than the open arms of Jesus on the cross, His arms are welcoming and invite shelter for those who need it, and hers are for purely self-serving and underhanded motives!

This book is the reality check for how things are handled in the REAL world. The struggles that have taken place while I am journeying through life, fighting for my daughters, Paris and Skyler. I have not given up,,,my thoughts, feelings and love for my girls, is just as strong or more as the day they were born.

As I sat in court, I was just beside myself, as if I was surrounded by more evil than one could comprehend. It was evil from my ex-wife's lies, her lawyer, and their hired expert that would validate whatever my ex-wife wanted him to say.

I knew instantly, no matter how much evidence I had or how unfit I proved Marlene to be, things were not going to end up for what was best for my girls. It was the biggest *"circus extravaganza"* of a hearing I've ever experienced, in three years, complete with clowns, the ring master, and the knife thrower. Too bad my back was the target. Not one person in the court room had the fear of God in them, except those who knew God.

That probably was the most amazing to me, it was just unbelievable at what was being said. After Marlene's lawyer questioned her on the stand, the court asked me if I had any questions for her. There was an overwhelming silence in the room, and I thought about it for a few minutes, while not a word was said by anyone. I'm sure the court and her lawyer expected a barrage of questions from me towards Marlene.

Then I said; *"I have one question"* your Honor for Marlene. I asked her; *"Have you ever seen me hurt my daughters or beat them?"* Marlene answered; **"NO"**. I said, "Your Honor, that is what started this entire custody hearing, she filed a false PPO on me claiming, I abused my daughters and they fear for their lives, that's why we're here in court three years later and I'm still fighting for the rights of my girls."

Six hours later after the custody hearing the motion for change of custody was denied. The court ordered the children to be supervised at all times by a competent adult under the mother's care, and that the mother shall not consume alcohol nor be intoxicated nor under the influence of illegal drugs in the presence of the children.

Did justice prevail for my children today? I believe so. The court ordered almost impossible rules on the mother. I have no doubts before my second book comes out she will violate this court order.

That's how God works. No one can be that wicked without God stepping in, and taking action. I believe that God influences the court in the end, on what to put in the order to keep the mother from drinking around our daughters, to give law enforcement a reason to keep Marlene in check and an eye on my girls.

Who knows, maybe this will wake up Marlene and she'll turn her life around, before she gets into any more trouble. Myself, I'm just astonished that she doesn't want to turn her life around and get out of the bars.

I find that such a waste of talent, Marlene does have a spiritual gift. Only if she would wake up and use it. Her bitterness in life, and the lifestyle she is living, is keeping her from her destiny. She is the mother of my children and I still hope the best of her.

I wish one day she would use her talents and pursue her spiritual gift. I want my daughters to be very proud of their mother. You have to remember in an instant, Marlene could change her life. All she has to do is ask God, and He will fill her with the Holy Spirit.

'What I Learned Under the Sun', is your prayers are always answered, you have to love like there's no tomorrow! Search your "heart", be "patient", and wait on the Lord. Never leave your kids behind. Fight for your children's rights and justice will prevail in the end. God's way and in His time.

The most important thing *'I Learned Under the Sun'*, is you can do whatever you want in life; there isn't anything that can hold you back from your dreams. No one can ever take your dreams from you and you'll always have those memories for a lifetime.

There isn't a night that goes by that I don't look at the stars and think of my girls. I know in my heart they're thinking of me. I dedicated this book to my girls and ironically the first proof was delivered to me on Saturday before Father's Day. The third Father's Day my ex-wife has kept my daughters from me. You truly can't get anymore evil than that as a mother.

What Marlene is doing is evil. You have to realize you can't blame her; she has no-clue what she is doing because she has hardened her heart. Your heart is the lifeline in your body, more so in ways, that it's almost impossible for us to comprehend. Everything you do comes from the heart, when you open up your heart and let the 'Holy Spirit' in, you'll find the meaning of true love under the sun.

Your heart is either filled with hatred or love; you walk in the light or the darkness. When you open up your heart the love pours in, your life will change instantly overnight. If you want to change your life, open up your heart. Then Miracles will start happening in your life. There isn't anything you can't do or accomplish under the sun.

'What I Learned Under the Sun', is Life has its ups and downs; you have to realize they're only for a moment in time. Keep the faith, because those issues that seem "devastating" are only a blessing that will bring you more joy and happiness than you could ever imagine, when you find your destiny under the sun!

'What I Learned Under the Sun', Lastly, no one can hold your kids hostage. Never, ever stop fighting for the rights of your children. Stand by them, stand up for them, always welcome them with open arms.

Big changes are ahead for our little family, new paths to follow, people to help, and lives to live under the sun . . . . See you in the next book because I have to prepare a place for my daughters under the sun!

God Bless,
TO BE CONTINUED

Index

Page 9

'What I Learned Under the Sun', is a unique memoir that relates the author's journey in life, love, and marriage.

'What I Learned Under the Sun', is my life story of blessings, that anyone can do whatever they want in life if one has faith, and all their dreams will come true.

'What I Learned Under the Sun', will inspire people looking for hope. That no matter how bad things seem, if you keep the faith, all the right doors will open up for you.

Page 10

'What I've Learned Under the Sun', is life isn't always fair, you better believe that you will reap what you sow, and the most important thing is, keeping the faith; no matter how bad things seem. God will open all the right doors for you and you will find your destiny under the sun!

Page 26

'What I learned Under the Sun', is people come into your life, leave a lot of happy memories that last forever.

Page 39

'*What I Learned Under the Sun*', is God places people together at the right moment in time. His timing is perfect!

Page 44

'*What I Learned Under the Sun*', is Love can't be bought, earned, or inherited. It's a gift from the Lord. If you wait on Him, He will bring you your soul mate (helpmate) in mind, body, and spirit.

Page 46

'*What I Learned Under the Sun*', is that random acts of kindness, comes from your heart.

Page 93

'*What I Learned Under the Sun*', is to have your sales double every year, you have to work with your buyers and the competition.

'*What I Learned Under the Sun*', is it's all about "honesty", being "humble", and that's how you make sales under the sun!

Page 125

'*What I Learned Under the Sun*', is whoever has the money always wins in court, it has nothing to do with what's right or wrong, money seems to always win.

Page 144

'*What I Learned Under the Sun*', is the day when I got home from court I had a letter from the new lawyer in Indianapolis; whom I had sent a proposal to, to handle my wage claim back in December. The firm basically guaranteed me a WIN by the end of the year on my wage claim.

Page 146

'*What I Learned Under the Sun*', is no matter what, you can never give up on your children, you have to fight for their rights, at all costs.

Page 150

'*What I Learned Under the Sun*', is signs from God are very real, when you have eyes that can see. The only requirement is you have to ask for a sign!

Page 153

'*What I Learned Under the Sun*', is that the Spirit is "Sensitive" to your thoughts and actions. When you realize your body is a temple of the Holy Spirit, who lives in you, whom you have received from God, your thoughts and ways change forever. The key is your heart!

Page 156

'*What I Learned Under the Sun*', is that when you turn from God to sin, and worship the devil, you become the devil's advocate, and then destruction follows.

Page 157

'What I Learned Under the Sun', is scripture is very real, the difference between a Proverbs 7 woman (Warning against the Adulteress), and the Proverbs 31 woman (Sayings of King Lemuel, "A wife of noble character who can find? She is worth far more than rubies."), is exactly as the Bible says it and its there for a reason!

Page 158

'What I Learned Under the Sun', is the hardest lesson in life is making the right choices. Regardless of how you try to present yourself or justify your sins, the truth will always come out in the end!

Page 159

'What I Learned Under the Sun', is Gods timing is perfect, He brought all the right people in place for my boss's success.

'What I Learned Under the Sun', is your actions come from within your heart, you have to guard your heart at all costs, that's reality. Jesus is the only way to heaven, and that's the ticket to heaven!

'What I Learned Under the Sun', is if you walk by faith, love always perseveres, love never fails. Trust in God even in the most difficult circumstances in your life, He will open up all the right doors for you. God uses pain and difficulties to draw us closer to Him, so we make changes in our lives.

'What I Learned Under the Sun', is you have to change your thoughts and that will determine your future. If you want to change your behavior you have to change the way you think!

Page 160

'*What I Learned Under the Sun*', is holding onto bitterness, is like a poison and it will eat you alive.

'*What I Learned Under the Sun*', is that holding onto that bitterness of poison, will take you down to the depths of hell; it shapes the outlook on your life, the kind of relationship you have, and how you treat your family and loved ones.

'*What I Learned Under the Sun*', is that the evil of bitterness will leave you in a dark state of being; you have no self-worth and it's emotionally paralyzing. If you live in darkness, it physically drains you and spiritually hardens your heart so you can't heal.

'*What I Learned Under the Sun*', is that your spiritual position and your eternal destiny are the only two things you know with certainty and no amount of money in the world can buy it.

'*What I Learned Under the Sun*', is there isn't a drug, drink, or high that can compare to the Holy Spirit in you.

Page 163

'*What I Learned Under the Sun*', is if someone in authority wants to put you in jail, they can put you there, and there isn't a thing you can do about it until you are released.

'*What I Learned Under the Sun*', is everything happens for a reason under the sun, it's the will of God why things happen, you just have to have faith in God's plan.

Page 164

'What I Learned Under the Sun', is a man reaps what he sows. Our actions, good or bad, have consequences. We *"reap"* the consequences of the deeds we have done.

Page 170

'What I Learned Under the Sun', is you better do everything in your 'POWER' to keep your children out of the court system, that is probably the most important advice I could give any loving parent. Families better start coming together, becoming self-sufficient and stop relying on the system.

Page 181

'What I Learned Under the Sun', is I always come out smelling like a rose!

'What I Learned Under the Sun', is we encounter a situation that appears hopeless, totally beyond our ability to handle; then God removes one obstacle after another, most of which we cannot explain, as we enjoy remarkable success.

Page 185

'What I Learned Under the Sun', is everything that happens under the sun happens for a reason. Guess what, now I'm married to her again! All I can say is; "Holy Smokes!"

Page 193

'What I Learned Under the Sun', is Divorce is just plain evil, now I know why God hates it!

Page 196

'What I learned Under the Sun', is it was a true blessing, Marlene didn't go to Las Vegas with me, and I didn't give her the money. It took every penny to pay legal fees or she would have succeeded with her evil plan of putting me back in jail the third time.

Page 199

'What I Learned Under the Sun', is that God will always give you a sign when you ask for one. I have also learned under the sun, that God will use other people to disclose to you what and why things are happening in your life. Nothing is hidden under the sun!

Page 201

'What I Learned Under the Sun', is all you have to do is keep the faith, and wait patiently, no matter what the problems are, everything works out in the end.

'What I Learned Under the Sun', is it's all about love, it's within all of us, and it's in your HEART. That is the secret under the sun; your heart is the key and when you turn from sin, the Lord will soften your heart, and overwhelm you with the joy of the Holy Spirit.

Page 202

'What I Learned Under the Sun', is when you praise God, that's when miracles start happening in your life.

Page 204

'What I Learned Under the Sun', is when you get a sign from the Lord nothing is impossible.

Page 206

'What I Learned Under the Sun', is everything happens for a reason and nothing is hidden under the Sun!

Page 207

'What I Learned Under the Sun', is that true faith is the ability to believe and trust in God in the midst of suffering. Wait patiently for Him, pray, and then believe in a miracle to happen in your life and it will.

'What I Learned Under the Sun', is faith cannot be trusted until it has been tested. My faith was tested many times and "you have to have faith even against seemingly insurmountable odds."

'What I Learned Under the Sun', is God uses people for His purpose in many ways. He knew He could use me because of my strength and faith.

Page 209

'What I Learned Under the Sun', is that no matter how bad things get, never, never give up and keep the faith. In no time at all, miracles will start happening in your life. Follow your heart, search out your dreams; anything can be accomplished under the sun!

Page 213

'What I Learned Under the Sun', is "Hatred is not an emotion that comes naturally to a child. It has to be taught. A parent who would teach her children to hate the other parent represents a grave and persistent danger to the mental and emotional health of that child."

Page 221

'What I Learned Under the Sun', is your prayers are always answered, you have to love like there's no tomorrow! Search your "heart", be "patient", and wait on the Lord. Never leave your kids behind. Fight for your children's rights and justice will prevail in the end. God's way and in His time.

Page 222

'What I Learned Under the Sun', is Life has its ups and downs; you have to realize they're only for a moment in time. Keep the faith, because those issues that seem "devastating" are only a blessing that will bring you more joy and happiness than you could ever imagine, when you find your destiny under the sun!

'What I Learned Under the Sun', Lastly, no one can hold your kids hostage. Never, ever stop fighting for the rights of your children. Stand by them, stand up for them, always welcome them with open arms.

To contact
Kyle L. Coon

I would love to hear from everyone that reads my book
and what you thought of it!

Write me at my e-mail address at **kylecoon4sales@aol.com** or leave me a message on my Author Page at **www.kylecoon.com**

See you in my next book, *"What I Did Under The Sun©."*

Edwards Brothers,Inc!
Thorofare, NJ 08086
24 November, 2010
BA2010329